# ENDORSEMENTS FOR

## NOT SO BY MYSELF:

*A safe space where God doesn't fix the loneliness, but sits with you instead*

One of the biggest lies we've learned to embrace is that we're alone in our pain. It keeps us trapped in a cycle of guilt, shame, and isolation so that even when we're struggling, we know how to put on a brave face and pretend everything is just fine. Peyton Garland is here for exactly none of that. She has lived with the agony of isolation, both physically and mentally, and is here to show us that just when we think we can't make it another second, there will always be a hope we can hold on to. With her approachable sense of humor and deeply rooted faith, Peyton offers us a way through our pain by sharing her own powerful story of redemption.

—**Wendi Nunnery**, author of *Good Enough: Learning to Let Go of Perfect for the Sake of Holy*

***

I LOVE IT! Peyton's honest, gritty truth of living with OCD, coping in a world of perfection, and "God are you there" moments ring authentic and powerful. I could relate on so many levels as a woman who struggles with perfectionism in my own life. I'm thrilled to know I'm not alone. This book is a must-read.

—**Shari Rigby**, author of *Consider the Lilies*, inspirational speaker, actress, and founder of The Women in My World.

*\*\*\**

Having had the chance to sit down across the table from Peyton and get to know her better, I can tell you confidently that she is for you. She is a cheerleader, already on the sidelines of your story- ready to root you on as you push further into what God has for you. Get ready to journey with her through the highs and lows of what it looks like to chase after God, deal with loneliness, and learn how to sit in the often-uncomfortable rhythms of faith and trust. There is a beauty and a transformation that only comes from learning to become comfortable with the uncomfortable - Peyton has been through that transformation and this book is proof.

—**Hannah Brencher**, author of *If You Find This Letter: My Journey to Find Purpose Through Hundreds of Letters to Strangers* and *Come Matter Here*, TED Talk speaker, and founder of The World Needs More Love Letters.

*\*\*\**

Peyton Garland is a compassionate friend to those suffering with loneliness, self-doubt, fear, anxiety, scary thoughts, and messy lives. She bravely shares her own journey through debilitating loneliness, her attempts to fix it on her own, then finally finding out that she had who she needed all along. Peyton's story is life changing. She is relatable, honest, raw, real, and funny. She has a gift for storytelling that draws the reader to experience life along with her. I appreciated her honesty about her struggles with God, her desperate prayer, and the insights He gave her while sitting in the lonely with Him. Life is messy! Peyton encourages us that we are not alone in our mess. God is always with us, comforting us, healing us, and leading us. Thank you, Peyton, for inviting us to glean from your life. It has encouraged me in my loneliness, strengthened me in my faith and increased my compassion for others who are struggling alone.

—**Janette Henning**, author of *Melissa, If One Life…*

*\*\*\**

I love the way Peyton writes; with such humanity and humility. She bravely shares her own trials and tribulations that makes a conversation about faith all the more relatable. Her honesty sets an example of how we should be with ourselves, with God, and with each other, because through that kind of communication, there is understanding, and understanding leads to choice, and choice is at the heart of faith.

—**Shaan Sharma**, actor in *The Chosen* and *Grey's Anatomy*, producer

# NOT SO BY MYSELF:

*A safe space where God doesn't fix the loneliness, but sits with you instead*

PEYTON GARLAND

Published by KHARIS PUBLISHING, imprint of KHARIS MEDIA LLC.

Copyright © 2020 Peyton Garland

ISBN-13: 978-1-946277-80-0
ISBN-10: 1-946277-80-0

Library of Congress Control Number: 2020920774

All Scriptural references are from the English Standard Version (ESV), unless noted otherwise.

All KHARIS PUBLISHING products are available at special quantity discounts for bulk purchase for sales promotions, premiums, fund-raising, and educational needs. For details, contact:

Kharis Media LLC
Tel: 1-479-599-8657
support@kharispublishing.com
www.kharispublishing.com

# DEDICATION

*I would like to dedicate this book to my Maw Maw, Bonnie.*

*Thank you for believing in me and my story long before I did.*

# CONTENTS

# ACKNOWLEDGMENTS

First and foremost, I would like to thank Jesus for being such a selfless God, the kind of God Who hands my most selfish dreams to me. Forever, He is good.

To my husband, Josh, thank you for believing in me. You always challenge me to better my writing skills, and all the while, you're cheering me on. I'm so grateful to call you my life partner.

Mom, Dad, Maw Maw, and Livie, even at my worst, you somehow see me as my best self. Thank you for a kind of love that I can always count on.

Pepa, I have a feeling that there's a huge library in heaven. If there is, I'd love for you to read this book.

Wendi, thank you for your bravery and vulnerability. If it wasn't for you (and a yucky matcha green tea), I wouldn't know that it's okay to give yourself grace as you fight a mental health disorder.

Jordin, Keren, Ryn, Tori, and Shayla, if it wasn't for your constant friendship, I wouldn't be half the woman I am. You're the best friends a girl could ever have.

Mary, my editor, thank you for championing my story. You are truly a kindred spirit.

Alfie and Daisy, my slobbering sausage balls, thank you for being there for me every night while Josh was away. You're my favorite furry nightmares.

# Introduction

I didn't want to pick up the dirty socks on his side of the bed. Sure, he would only be gone for five days this time, but I was afraid I would wash, dry, fold, and put away any proof he shared a bedroom with me.

I couldn't walk downstairs to the dark basement, either. I had several decorations in storage containers I needed to bring upstairs and hang on the walls, but those were surrounded by his tools, golf balls, and work gloves that he was never home to use. If I stood there long enough, I could feel the dank chill coming up from the cement floor, working its way into my heart.

The kitchen became a strange land because food took third place to anxiety and exhaustion. The living room became a place of survival, where I occupied the center. I was unsure how to kill an entire afternoon, until I had stood by the chaise, frozen long enough to do just that.

I lost weight-- too much weight. My walking heart rate blew past 130 BMP. Tremors overtook my hands so vigorously that I would have spilled my coffee if it hadn't had a top on it. Stress knots twisted my neck muscles, causing my posture to lean and hunch over like Quasimodo's.

It was as if Josh, my husband, had died and taken my life with him.

But he was alive, breathing, pulsing, living much healthier than I was.

My new job had toted us to Roswell, Georgia, too far from any of my family for a decent post-work visit. And less than a month after we moved, Josh's career carried him eight hours away from me. This separation wasn't a one-time business trip or a two-week conference. As a newbie pilot, he was stationed at whichever airport he'd been assigned. He couldn't come home for good until a new position opened up in an airport in Atlanta. For four months, I faced a new city, a new job, a new neighborhood, and a new house alone. I'll be the first to say it was hell, pure hell.

For the first time in my life, God had guided me to a place where I couldn't run to the security of my family. I couldn't duck behind my laptop in my favorite coffee shop. I couldn't hang out down the street with my neighbor who always asked about my dogs.

I was alone, soon alone with a woman I no longer knew, although she wore my skin.

I was emotionally abusing myself, believing the lie that God's fix-all button was controlled by my accomplishments and completed checklists. I was emotionally abusing God, hoping if I were good enough or mad enough or pitiful enough, He would have to say, "Okay, Peyton, I can't see you hurt like this anymore. Let me map out this whole mess for you so Josh can come on home."

This cycle brought zero answers, zero peace.

Praise be to the God of all things good; I am now on the other side of this trench and Josh is home. Looking back, though, I can say now I understand why God let me wander through loneliness, much as the Israelites wandered through the desert. He let me sit in my lonely place because that loneliness was my safe space. It was the one place where God knew I would be able to hear Him, the one place where I could be raw and real, without the threat of Him leaving me.

Will this hindsight and insight make new bouts of loneliness any easier? Probably not, but I have been given a new perspective I can cling to until eternity. I am certain of that.

After all, I'm kidding myself if I think loneliness won't throw me in the boxing ring again for round two later on. I can't -- none of us can -- stroll through this life without friendships breaking, dogs running away, loved ones dying, and all the other sad things that leave us crying on the bathroom floor.

But I'm here, ready to sit with women who forget to visit the kitchen and feed themselves. I'm here for women who are scared to walk into a dark, messy bedroom that whispers, "You're all by yourself." I'm here for women who are trying to distract their loneliness with so much noise that their days feel like they're spinning. I'm here, with you in your lonely mess. If you'll sit with me through all these pages, you'll realize that Someone much cooler than I am is here. He's with you in the mess because He works best in the mess. He's not going anywhere, and because of Him, you're not so by yourself.

# Dog Park Drama

Have you ever gotten out of bed, spotted the sunshine, smelled the roses (or your lavender air freshener plug-in), and said, "Yep, I'm going to make today a good day!"?

Have you ever said that, only to have it followed by such cascading tragic events as:

Spilling coffee on the crotch of your pants just one red light away from the office?

Realizing you haven't fed the dogs since yesterday, or maybe the day before?

Forgetting that you were supposed to cancel your Hello Fresh® membership before they charged you another forty dollars for those healthy purple onions you don't even like?

As for me and my house, the answer is yes to all of the above. Ninety-nine percent of the time, I am a planner, the Super Woman Scheduler. I always have every minute of every day mapped out, despite low-key denial that life doesn't follow my nanosecond-by-nanosecond itinerary. Since I map out high expectations for a good day each day, and since I still forget random things, I end up with sticky pants and the loss of $40 I could've spent on new pillows instead of purple onions. I map out my day precisely, but reroute my day out of frustration, worry, and stress.

Most days, by around 5:30, I've made it home from work. More than likely, I've already stopped by Kroger® to pick up the dog food I forgot the day before. I've convinced myself that I needed a Starbucks™ Iced Green Tea with three packs of melted honey instead of liquid cane. By 6:30, I have already confessed to my husband which coworker might be mad at me because they did not talk to me by the coffee station that day. I've also asked him to check my temperature for reassurance that I haven't brought home the flu, stomach bug, or coronavirus. Like I said, I operate out of worry, but my worries, anxieties, and clinical Obsessive-Compulsive Disorder (OCD) kicks are a little quieter when I can dump them on another human.

Is this the healthiest way to handle my problems? No. Does Josh enjoy the fact that all I do is unload my qualms on him, then find more problems to pack on? No. Do I still handle craziness my own way, apologize to God that night, and then handle craziness my own way again the next day? *Mmhmm*.

I got by on this faulty system for a little while, but Josh's rookie piloting career shipped him from Atlanta, Georgia to New Albany, Indiana to Tampa, Florida for four months. Then my barely self-sufficient cycle of handling stress broke. I had no one to assure me I was overthinking why so-and-so didn't talk to me at the coffee bar. There was no one to take my temperature and convince me I didn't have Ebola, Lyme Disease, or a rare heart condition. There was nowhere to dump my worries, stresses, biggest fears, and little hissy fits. And in case you're like me and math isn't your thing, here's the simple equation that mapped out my problem: (No one to talk to + nothing to blame all situations on) x (nowhere to run) = me

And "me" is lonely, stressed, scared Peyton.

Usually, this is when most women would get coffee with a friend, but we had just moved to a new neighborhood in a new city for my job. All my friends were hours away in my hometown. And, as my US Army veteran father said, "People don't need to know that you're by yourself. Don't worry, I'll bring my work truck up there and park it by your car so somebody thinks there's a man in the house." I thought it safest if I parked my car under the carport, ran inside the house, locked the door behind me, and turned on all the lights so it looked like I was always having some sort of faux *Home Alone* party.

This is when most employees would confide in a co-worker, but like I said, I was the new girl. I didn't have a feel for who to trust or whose personality clicked with mine. Besides, I was too focused on staying quiet and mapping the fastest route to the office bathroom.

2

This is when most daughters would call their mom and sob, but
to pour my whole life on her. She's already done her fair sh'
Kelly had already dealt with me for twenty-five years and had more ᵥ.
signed a lifelong contract to tolerate me for at least another five decades. God
bless her patience.

This is when most Christians would, could, should call on God, but friends,
here's my secret: I suffer with OCD, so talking to God triggers some random,
scary thoughts in my head. Weird much? This is so much more than wanting
all the soup can labels facing out. It's way more than straightening crooked
picture frames and demanding an even number of chairs around the dinner
table. For those of you who are unfamiliar with the clinical details, I primarily
suffer with two of the four branches of Intrusive Thought OCD: 1) Contamination and Hand-washing and 2) Taboo Thoughts and Mental Rituals.

How does this look? How does it make me look? I come off as a super ger-
maphobe who is constantly afraid I've damned myself to hell. Most people
can shrug off their random, weird thoughts about how germs spread; most
people don't freak out when the last three digits of their credit card are the
apocalyptic number that we will not discuss, but OCD doesn't allow my
body's adrenaline to taper off. I live perpetually in this "fight-or-flight" response readiness. I have the most bizarre thoughts and can't talk myself down
from them. For me, talking to God might mean I accidentally think something really bad about Him and then *poof!* He up and leaves me.

(Side note: If you know someone who has been diagnosed with OCD, please
call them right now. I'm not kidding. Put down this book because it'll still be
here when you get back. Let them know that the God of all good things has
redeemed every piece of their mind, and that because of God, no crazy
thoughts or obsessions will redefine the beauty God sees in them.)

Now, I was always the good Christian girl who walked all the fine lines. Count
my Awana trophies; I could smoke Simone Biles' Olympic Gold Medal
count. I hung onto my virginity until I was married. I gasped in horror when
someone had the audacity to wear a mini skirt to church, but I toed these fine
lines, most of them self-drawn, out of fear of God, not out of His grace. It
has taken me 13 years to grapple with the idea that God is really good and
doesn't bail on people when they do the slightest thing wrong. Still, when I
am in doubt or I am lonely, I resort to terror and don't talk to Him, don't

3

read my Bible, don't do anything to focus my entire attention on Him. Why? Because if I do, I might say, think, or do something bad.

After all, why talk to God when I'm scared or lonely, when I'm more likely to say whatever raw, mean things I'm thinking? Why read the Bible if its words might confuse me or make me wonder why I believe what I believe? And, hello, who wants to anger the God Who has a rep for turning folks into pillars of salt?

Instead of letting God unearth the parts of me that weren't so tidy, I dumped my problems on Josh. He became a safer space where I could flesh out all my craziness, because he couldn't erase my name from *The Book of Life*. Also, I had never seen Josh Garland powerful enough to call a pack of bears from the mountains to maul a group of people who made fun of a bald prophet named Elisha. I mean, who would I rather upset here? The God with the bears or Josh Garland, who still asks me where I put his Aqua Man briefs?

One day, only a few weeks after Josh left, I couldn't sit alone, stare at a wall, and face down the scared me I'd been running from. Rather than phoning a human or, geez, I don't know, talking with Jesus, I decided to take my two tail-wagging youngsters, Alfie and Daisy, to the dog park.

Dog parks sound fun, look fun, and if you ignore the dog poo, they smell fun. Fair warning, my canine-loving friends: This is just sensory deception that tricks you into locking yourself in chain-linked, furry chaos. It morphs you into that mom who can't make her four-legged children behave in public.

Before the rest of this story unfolds, understand that my two furry children are absolute gremlins. Alfie, my two-year-old, 75-pound brindle, is nothing but selfish slobber that drools on whatever he wants, whenever he wants. He couldn't care less if you dangled 500 treats in his face; if he doesn't want to come to you, he's not coming. You can spank him, take away his chew toys, put him in timeout, but it doesn't matter. He lives life the way he sees fit.

Daisy, my white and brown-speckled, 55-pound baby girl is a crazy sausage ball. She has a lazy eye, a disproportionately thick torso, and is terrified I will one day love another dog more than her. You can pet her for days on end and validate your love for her with the dearest words of affirmation, but she doesn't care. Daisy Girl has to know that she's your number one.

At this point, you're probably asking why I would take these two nightmares to the dog park. Let me reiterate: Loneliness, panic, and the threatened dread of sitting in an empty house for hours on end drove me to do some wild things.

Shocker! Alfie and Daisy don't do well on leashes, and I'm a small chick, weighing in at a mean 110 pounds. Add their weight together and it's clear what happened. They dragged me across the perilous parking lot full of rushed soccer moms telling their wide-eyed husbands, "Just hurry up and park!"

By God's grace, I made it inside the chain-link fence of this fancy, fake-turfed dog park. I yanked the leashes off the dogs' collars and set them free. Since I overthink conversations with strangers, I found an empty bench, positioned myself to give off the "Don't sit beside me" vibe, and thanked myself for getting some herbal tea before arriving.

I had not been seated for five minutes, perhaps five seconds, before I heard a pack of ferocious barks. I had lost my dogs in the sea of other slobbering sausage balls running around, so I missed Alfie deciding he had the hots for a poor, three-legged, female dog. He proceeded to do the dirty in front of everyone, and in the process, started a total riot amongst other alpha male dogs.

> *Please don't let that be one of mine! Please don't let that be one of mine!* I thought as I raced across the park toward the dog pile.

Other dog owners were yanking their pets from the mound, and lo and behold, when the other minor offenders were ripped away, there was my Alfie, the ringleader of this monstrosity. Dog fur was everywhere. The poor three-legged dog was bleeding from the gums and her whole black and tan body shook. And there I was, the already-wound-up, worried self-shamer who had to apologize to a ton of strangers and a tripod dog that would never understand what just happened.

Needless to say, we didn't stay at the dog park. Enough people had made ugly faces at me and made snide, loud comments about my irresponsible lack of control over my dog, so I knew it was my cue to leave. I didn't want to take Alfie and Daisy back home with me, but I didn't want to go to jail for animal cruelty by abandoning them. What choice did I have in the matter?

5

By the time I finagled them into the car and fought traffic to get home, it was dark. Most stores were getting ready to close. Most people were hunkering down for the night. I sat on my couch and replayed my traumatic experience, wondering why my plan, meant only to distract me from loneliness, had failed so miserably.

Here's the kicker: My question held the answer. Distractions don't work. I mean, they might seem to go well in the short-term. After all, I enjoyed those ten seconds of absolute bliss as my dogs ran off to play and I managed to gulp down three sips of my tea, but reality swooped in and rounded off the day. It was like Spotify© commercials, electric bills, and dirty laundry, all things we can try to ignore for a little while, but they eventually get really big and loud. They pile up all over your life and you can't stay away from them forever. Plus, you could wind up naked on the side of the road with no good music to listen to. Stuff gets bad really fast, but, as humans, rather than sitting with God and wrestling with the lonely, messed up pieces of ourselves, we like to cram our schedules with lots of loud distractions. That's when things go from bad to worse:

Your boyfriend's pretty words might distract you from how much you hate your body, but when he goes home, it's late at night, and it's time for you to take a shower, you still have to face your pimples, your stretch marks, your gray hairs, and those pieces of you that make you an imperfect human, like the rest of us.

Your job title might distract you from past failures and keep you busy enough to focus on paperwork and the people you get to boss around, but when 5:01 p.m. hits each day, you're stuck by yourself on that lovely commute home. Afternoon radio talk shows are annoying, so you're better off inside the quiet.

The dog park might have distracted me from how lonely I was, but after that inappropriate scene with Alfie and poor Tripod, I had to come home to an empty, dark house. I had to deal with how I saw me, how I saw God, and how I was afraid to wrestle with that all alone. I had to return to nothing, nothing but isolation and nobody but God. At first, and by "at first," I mean for a long, long time, that was uncomfortable. I didn't want to sit alone with my thoughts and feelings, trying to guard them from a God Who could still hear and see all life was pouring on me. But that was my reality, the one I had to sit with. And at some point, it's the one we all have to sit with.

Here's some good news, though: There's a little light for you and me at the end of this grayish tunnel. While the situation with Josh being gone never got easier, sitting with loneliness got easier. It was not because God wrote, "PEY-TON, JOSH WILL BE HOME BY JANUARY 9TH AND ALL WILL BE WELL," on the wall, nor yelling that with clouds of smoke crashing. Instead, God used loneliness to fix my lonely. There was so much lonely, so many stresses, and so many failures, that I was too tired to gab on the phone with Josh through my problems. I was too tired to distract myself. All I had the energy to do was say, "God, I can't. I just can't anymore... Please just stay."

And this prayer, one of the least profound prayers in the history of all pretty prayers, became one of the biggest turning points in my relationship with Him. It was a prayer I would have never said, had I not sat all alone, had the loneliness not made me face fear and stress and, well, face myself.

I can't promise you that God will part the Red Sea of cars on your way to work so you don't slam on your brakes and spill coffee on your crotch. There's no guarantee that dog food manna will fall from the sky and land in Fido's bowl, but God will do lots of talking and lots of showing up in your life if you'll sit in the lonely and spill out whatever words you can offer Him.

The good thing is this: Even though He's not banking on how well you handle solitude and the monsters that creep out from under your bed, you can bank on Him. Things do get better because it isn't God who supplies us with distractions. He supplies us with the good stuff that stays, with His promises that can't be broken, and with His love that guarantees us that we really aren't ever all alone. And if we know that God's Spirit is filling every little cranny of our past, present, and future, we can face anything, literally anything, knowing that what will sustain us isn't a lack of sin, a lack of mess-ups, and a flawless inability to cope with an ever-changing, ridiculously stressful life. Rather, what will sustain us is His goodness that will forever keep our hearts bound to Him.

# Preserved

Loneliness feels vastly empty when you realize that unsure things have been the confines of your unsteady safe place. Even as a child, a teenager, a student, before I knew that it was OCD gripping my thoughts, my brain was always so loud, especially with things I didn't like, things that weren't truly me. I was willing to fight for any title, be anyone's friend, and host all of the sleepovers to seem normal, likeable, and cool. I was willing to belong anywhere if it meant something or someone else might steady my feet, quiet my head, and shield me from solitude.

Back in good ol' 2012, I graduated as valedictorian of my high school class. It's quite the title to reminisce on during family reunions or to showboat when I'm trying to one-up my husband's wit. It's one of those things that you still try to sneak in your resume too, even though you have a graduate degree. Nobody in corporate America cares anything about anything you did as an 18-year-old unless you committed a federal offense and went to prison for it. They'll want that information, guaranteed. By the way, valedictorians can't go to jail. It's not in our tightrope-walking nature. The only illegal thing I ever did in high school was jaywalk through a cemetery and leave flowers on a random person's grave.

What I didn't tell clueless Aunt Peggy at the family reunion, though, was that there were only 13 people in my graduating class. THIRTEEN. You almost have enough fingers to check off every cap and gown that marched across that stage. One of the 13 students was from South Korea and still hadn't mastered every aspect of the English language, so he didn't really count in the valedictorian race. So, there were 12 of us, leaving only 11 kids for me to beat for the title. As always, there was a class clown who only showed up to make jokes, a couple of jocks who thought they needed just enough A's to play collegiate golf, and maybe three or four of us who actually cared to know what G-P-A stood for.

I wasn't smart, not by any means, especially in math, science, and anything to do with numbers. I didn't like formulas, I couldn't understand equations, and I refused to pair evil numbers with beautiful letters to form word problems. Regardless, I studied and cried, and ate ten chicken nuggets, then I studied and cried some more. I went to Starbucks™ and chugged Passion Tea, never slept, and by Jesus' grace, held the top GPA in my class.

Obviously, I had to speak at graduation, which at the time seemed pretty special. I wore an extra gold cord, someone gave me a feature page in the yearbook, and then, a few days after we tossed our caps, nobody cared. Including me. Sure, I throw around the title when it'll get me five seconds of fame, but does anyone really care about my Physical Science and American History scores from a decade ago? I hope not.

But more than GPAs and gold cords, I think people like titles because they make us feel like we belong somewhere, like we naturally have other valedictorian friends. When I graduated, Georgia's governor invited me and every other 2012 valedictorian in the state to come to a luncheon at his house, and *voila!* I had instant friends. We didn't have to talk at the finger food table. I didn't have to follow them on Facebook when the luncheon was over. But all of us knew that we liked each other because at least one of the niches in our lives intersected. If every other aspect of my 18-year-old world had crumbled, if volleyball had ceased to exist, and if all my One Act Play medals were stripped away, I wouldn't have cared that day. I now had hundreds of smarty pants friends. I still had a place where I fit in and that was what mattered.

And that's what still matters. Adults find cliques and niches and stay super loyal to their people. We don't like being by ourselves or feeling like we aren't cool enough to be liked, so we flock to people who function the same way we do so we are validated, viewed as normal, and well-preserved.

Granted, we aren't 12 years old anymore, buying each other matching lip glosses and making up code names for the boys we liked, but don't tell me you aren't overladen with joy when your best friend has memorized your overly complicated Starbucks™ order. Don't act like you don't have encrypted emoji codes that you use as an SOS when you're texting your friends in the middle of an awkward, crummy date. For the most part, we like these special orders and codes. They give us an identity that's only important because someone else cared enough to memorize it. When enough of us join forces and create group texts with inside joke names and weekly Zoom® dates, we've reached the pinnacle of belonging somewhere. And we prefer to belong somewhere for good, to be preserved.

"Preserved" is such a pretty word. "Preserved" sounds safe, like I'm locked up tight in this gold jar full of black confetti, books, Justin Bieber, green tea, dogs, and all the other things I like. But preserving your status, preserving you just as you are, is never safe. In fact, it's stagnant. It's dangerous, and instead of simply appreciating Justin Bieber's tattoos or enjoying reading a book, we unknowingly begin to worship and obsess over these things because they keep our routine level. They keep things safe as they are, giving us no room to feel boxed out.

We can go to a JB concert because there will be thousands of other screaming crazies just like us, or we can bust into our favorite coffee shop and surround ourselves with other book nerds. We can validate our actions, our desires, our everything, via people. If someone else is doing life the same way we are, then all lights are green and we must be doing things right. Right?

When Josh left for four months, I couldn't concentrate long enough to read a book. I didn't have the energy to turn on Justin Bieber's latest album and chunk black confetti around the living room, and the dogs were a chore. I couldn't open any stinking jar in the house, whether it was a sparkly gold one or a jar of spaghetti sauce. It was hard to fit in and connect with people; I had zero desire to plug in anywhere. While that seems like a curse, to be without group chats and coffee dates, it was quite the blessing for me.

Being so alone, I had to figure me out, without any of the extra tags, without any of the titles, hobbies, or friend groups. I had to be that middle school girl who ate at the lunch table by herself every single day of first semester, except I couldn't hide out and eat my lunch in the bathroom. There was no sneaking off to a classroom. No matter which room in my house I could've chosen, I still had to face the isolating bully called Loneliness.

It sounds tiring. It was tiring. It still is tiring when I try to take that same lifeless route of spinning my wheels, going nowhere at 90 miles an hour.

The problem was, I was approaching loneliness in the same exhausting way I had taken off after my valedictorian title. I was working. *Hard.* Way too hard, but with an end goal that wouldn't fix anything long-term. I was hoping that valedictorian title would mean something lasting, something that would always make me feel like I had a right to occupy space in the busiest of rooms. In my first semester of college, though, no one cared about anything or anyone from high school, especially the person who was nerdy enough to obsess over school work for four years. I was begging for titles, people, groups, and all the things to stay and make me feel like I wasn't by myself, even though it was not within my power to call those shots. It is still not within my power.

I can't force friend groups to stay intact. I've been in and out of enough life phases to realize that people constantly come and go, and it's not my place to control who goes when and where. Your best friend goes to a different college and suddenly, long distance drastically changes things. Your best friend gets married. Now, her husband is her best friend and the third wheel is a little too wobbly and squeaky to hang on. Your best friend has a new baby and is too mind numb and sleep deprived to realize she never texted you back. You can't bank on friends fulfilling you. Not that they can't minister to you and bless you, but you have no firm grip on your relationships; at least, your grip is not tight enough to force people to stay in your life forever.

I can't even force Justin Bieber to drop a new album. I can't make him produce new music to drown out my own thoughts, once I can mindlessly repeat every lyric of every song from every previous album. Doesn't matter how loud I blare the speakers or how wild of a solo dance party I host in my living room, I can't make a three-minute tune nurture me through a lonely, grueling 24-hour day.

All of the fun Peyton things that I crammed in my gold jar just shoved my problem with myself deeper and deeper into my soul. For the most part of my life, I always knew I was using this falsified preservation concept to only push me a few days further down the road. I was just using the coffee date to get me through a breakup, using books as an escape from the drama in my own life. These things that made me "belong" were supposed to solve my problems, but in life, the hurdles don't stop. I'll always need something outside of coffee and confetti to make me feel permanently safe, someone to make me feel like I belong somewhere for the rest of forever.

11

And as much of a Sunday School cliché as it is, that Someone is the Holy Spirit. While on earth, Jesus was the ultimate gorilla glue party host. It didn't matter if you were a prostitute, a leper, or the richest guy around; He recognized all of the lonely, hurt, sin-filled shards of thousands of hearts and invited everyone to crash at His place while He pieced them back together. He gave everyone a place where they belonged, even when these people weren't truly themselves, even when they were too confused, scared, angry, hurt, and lonely to even want to belong somewhere. Jesus knew we were utterly lonely without Him, that titles and friend groups and all the high points in life aren't enough to fix us. And when Jesus left earth, He gave the Holy Spirit the key to His place, where we can come while the Holy Spirit picks up our shards and glues us back together.

I'll be honest, it would be nice if Jesus fit into my 2020 definition of belonging. There's not a day in my life when I don't wish I had the Holy Trinity in a group message. I'd love to get coffee with them and say, "Hey, life sucks. Please help a girl out!"

It has taken a long time, and the sheer embarrassment of trial and error, for me to stop banking so much on people, awards, and temporary things. Yet, God is really good at making me feel like I'll always belong somewhere, even when I'm alone. In my loneliness, He's given me the space to realize that I've been worshipping everything that made me feel like I belonged, everything except Him. Despite the myriad "to-do" lists revolving around seven-billion people and trillions of galaxies, He makes plenty of room on His calendar for me, day in and day out.

I'm not saying the Christian life is easy and that you'll always feel God as closely as you would feel a 15-pound anxiety blanket, but it's just the knowing part. For me, it's knowing He's too kind to cram me into a jar of shallow things that keep me from realizing where I eternally belong. It's my knowing He's adventurous enough to force me outside of my titles and boxes, while He commands the winds and waves. He tells them to move over, to make room for His daughter, so I can keep trudging through the hard things and keep rejoicing in the good things.

My God is a Preserver, but sometimes He preserves in the loneliest and the wildest ways that crack all the corners where we've crammed ourselves.

I'm not always okay with being me, aside from my labels. There were, and are, many times I don't feel so comfortable in my own skin, but there is this little piece of my glued-up heart that constantly whispers, "You're safe. You belong. You're good." If you'll listen for that, it won't matter if you're President of the United States or President of the Girl Scout Mom Squad, you will belong. There will be no group messages or monogrammed bumper stickers required.

# The Look of Things

Even before Josh's flight dream existed, before his rainbows and unicorns career goal turned into my ibuprofen bottle and chiropractic visits, we could never avoid all things hectic. Eventually, I couldn't avoid being alone, either, even if it was just for one night.

Josh and I were in nail-biting, seat-clenching crunch time to find a house before we got married. Prior to the move to Roswell, we were scrambling for a house in Newnan, Georgia, the halfway point between both of our jobs.

I was always told to never buy into the credit card traps set for young folks, and I was also the powdered princess who never made her own car payments. The only things I ever purchased out of my own pocket were nuggets and coffee. So, guess who had zero credit and slowed down the entire house-buying process? Yup, me.

It was only a matter of weeks before our wedding day, and we knew living with our parents would not make for a decent, temporary residence. Really, who wants to have sex when their parents are across the hall? To our dismay, things looked much nicer online than they did in person. Somebody must be very good at taking pictures of awkward, boxy houses, because the online photographs never alluded to the make-or-break point where someone squeezed a half bath and a refrigerator into the same two-foot space. Discouraged after our third night of house hunting, Josh was ready to go home.

"What about that other little house?" I asked. "It's only a few miles from here. We might as well give it a shot."

We met our realtor about ten minutes later at this itty-bitty, yellow-trimmed, brick home. When we walked in, the 1980s screamed at us with loud, dingy carpet, patchy and poorly stained door frames, and rusted kitchen cabinets that would require a tetanus shot prior to use. Josh rolled his eyes when I gave him the, "This is what I want," look. There really wasn't much to the house. It only had one narrow bathroom, three tiny bedrooms, no back porch or back door. The fire code was a little sketch, and the yard needed lots of love. Nobody was fighting for the little place, so we had no fear of being outbid.

It took a second, but I realized my obsession with the place. It had the same old-time feel and the same layout as my Maw Maw and Pepa's house. When you walked inside, you were in a kitchen that immediately fed into the living room and a hallway full of bedrooms. In my book, that was enough for it to feel like home. After a small, "Is this house worth that much?" battle with Josh, I won. We made a measly offer that nearly murdered our bank account, the owner took us up on it, and the itty-bitty house was ours.

The dirty white walls were painted pretty blues, lavenders, and light greens. The carpet was ripped up and replaced with beautiful, brown, shiny laminate flooring, and the cabinet hinges and knobs were upgraded with a rust-resistant product. Pictures were hung, lamps were put in place, knick-knacks filled empty corners. My favorite books were nestled everywhere and candle scents filled every room. The place slowly turned from a house into our home. Everything was slowly falling into place, except there was one little detail about the lot that kept us up countless nights.

Our first house was on the corner lot that welcomed everyone into the neighborhood. It was visible from the main highway. We thought the little place would be a quick, easy access for our commutes to work; we'd be in and out of the neighborhood in five seconds. This little corner lot came with lots of people no one had told us about before we signed on the dotted line… lots of random, scary, stoned, highway people.

The first night that Josh was away, and I had to stay there alone, everything was going great. I was doing some deep cleaning, playing my favorite music, and totally forgetting how much I overthink everything. Out of nowhere, Alfie and Daisy started barking, the kind of barking that's more serious than chasing down a squirrel. I grabbed my little pink pistol and tiptoed out into our carport. It was ten o'clock at night and someone was at the end of my driveway. She was not in a car, not with someone else, just standing there alone. I was creeped out, but my military brat training pepped up a little confidence. I approached the woman and asked if she was looking for something.

She started talking ninety-to-nothing, but it was all gibberish. The only thing I caught was, "Can I just talk to you?" Even as a sheltered Christian school kid, I knew this poor woman was on something and was out of her mind.

*This is how I'm going to die*, I thought. *This is where it all ends for me, and I'm not even finished painting the kitchen...*

Somewhat annoyed, I did what I thought Jesus would want me to do. I nodded her towards a chair in my garage and quickly concealed my weapon. She reeked of the alcohol she was carrying in her coffee mug. Turns out, she lived on the other side of the highway, in a rundown house covered with torn rebel battle flags and shattered glass; it was a house I preferred to ignore. She told me she had recently been released from jail and came home, only to find her husband cheating on her. She was crying, snorting snot, and just looked like a train wreck; it was kind of the way I looked in the deepest part of my anxiety. Maybe that encounter was God's way of softening me up, tearing down pieces of my wary skepticism and predetermined judgment. I found ways to ask questions that would show me whether she was in physical danger. I also made sure she wouldn't be alone with her husband when she went back to that house.

After she rambled on for about 30 minutes, and I had talked myself into the notion that nobody was going to die, she wanted to come inside my house and look around. She told me she had wanted to buy my house when they moved across the street. Knowing this house wasn't even on the market when she came along, I let her inside. Every normal piece of me screamed,

*UH, WHAT ARE YOU DOING? SHE COULD STEAL SOMETHING OR PULL OUT A KNIFE. THEN YOU'RE SCREWED!*

She walked through the house, touching each of my pictures, gripping each doorframe, and asking me all sorts of questions about Josh's and my future plans for each room. She went in my bathroom, closed the door, and came out without flushing the toilet or turning on the faucet; I'm about 95 percent sure she was scrounging around for some prescription drugs. Eventually, she left my house without any meds and went back across the street. Once she was out of earshot, I called Mom and told her what happened.

16

"Baby, don't you ever do that again!" she said. "Next time, just call the police."

"I was just doing what I thought was right," I fumbled, knowing how stupid I sounded, throwing myself into a situation like this one.

"I know," Mom said, surprising me with a much calmer voice. "These are the people that Jesus didn't turn away."

I had zero clue what to do that night. All I could think was that it hadn't been my job to turn that woman away. I'm not sure why she went to jail. I'm not sure why she needed to carry alcohol in a coffee mug. I'm not sure if she even had a husband. What I am sure of is that it had not been my job to ignore her or pretend my life was better than hers. That was especially not the case when 90 percent of my life had been handed to me with lots of love and social capital.

That night, all alone for the first time since "I do," I was scared to go to sleep, but at the same time, I felt content. It's not always easy or safe to do what you're supposed to do. Honestly, it's rarely pure joy to serve others and let a doped-out stranger meander through your house. It was nothing so big and boisterous that warranted a medal, but it was somehow big enough that I knew I had put my life on the line. All the while, there was this weird satisfaction that came with fulfilling a piece of the Gospel, especially when I was lonely. I learned, if you're brave enough to do this the first time, it will happen again. And then again. And then again.

Not even a month after this fiasco, Josh and I were curled up on a Saturday night, binge watching tv. Out of nowhere, someone started beating, not knocking, beating on our door. "Help, man! You gotta call 9-1-1!" he panted over and over.

Ready for 75-pound Alfie to take his attack dog stance, I watched him whimper and back into the corner of our tv stand, instead.

*Geez, I'm just really trying to die this year,* I thought.

Josh bowed up, charged to the door, and flipped up our curtains.

"What's going on, buddy?" he ordered.

This teenage boy was too stoned for Josh to make sense of the details. All the boy knew was that he needed medical attention. He was roughed up, no doubt, but Josh kept us inside until the local sheriff's deputy showed up.

"You guys were probably the only ones with a light on in your house," the officer said. "That's why he picked y'all. He probably got into some gang trouble and cut through the woods a few neighborhoods over and ran onto your property. We'll send him to the hospital and get him checked out."

When yours is the first house on the corner, the one that stands out with a bright porch light, folks just run to you.

I think that's why people are attracted to Jesus. Maybe that's why Jesus calls Himself the Light. Perhaps there's a reason that we are called the light in the dark too. God is just waiting there with a bright light and a front door sign that reads, "You're safe here." This kind of warmth fills us up when the world has left us stumbling in the dark. It's attractive, not because of the "sell everything you have" part, but because you know, when life is hard, even when living out Christianity is hard, you always belong somewhere. There's always this big God Who promises to lead you to safety, and that's worth giving up everything else.

About two months after the teenager showed up at our door, we were getting ready to jet for one of those insane Saturdays when you know you're going to get zero rest. Josh had a flight to make. I had errands to run. He had to find a belt. I had calories to lose, and we both had to meet my family for breakfast. As usual, we overslept and were running more than a minute or two behind. Just as we locked our door and took off towards the Prius®, this guy in a black skull hoodie yelled our way, "Hey, man! Do you have a gas can we could borrow?"

*WHAT GIVES?!* my mind bellowed.

Skull Hoodie and his hefty, five o'clock shadow friend had pushed their small silver car into the back corner of our property. It was 100% out of gas, with just smoke and fumes puffing out.

After traipsing around our dirty garage, Josh found an old gas can without a nozzle and gave it to Skull Hoodie. I tried to shake off "self" just long enough to be helpful. "Josh, why don't we just drive up the road and fill up the can ourselves?" I proposed.

Part of me didn't have the heart to watch them walk up the road in the cold weather, and the other part of me wanted to watch them exit our property without taking an extra tv along for the trip.

Josh and I drove less than a third of a mile to the nearby gas station, filled up the small can for only two dollars, and brought the gas back to the sketchy guys.

"Hey, God bless, man! Thank you so much!" they said.

They tried to pay us back, but my husband was too kindhearted for that. We let them keep the can for the next time they mistakenly assumed they could make it another ten miles. We watched them leave our property, waving their thanks as they went.

"That really is a God thing, ya' know," Josh said as we headed to breakfast an extra 20 minutes late.

*A God thing?* my brain fumed.

But once my brain calmed down (again) and I let Jesus take over my thought patterns, I started thinking that maybe that was what the boy meant when he said, "God bless, man!" I doubt we will ever get a random $10,000 check in the mail for our little charitable deed, even though that would pay off the car and be really cool. Instead, maybe the blessing was how content Josh and I felt living on this little corner lot. We didn't have a lot of money. Seriously, I cringed when Josh waved away their attempt to pay us back… for a whole two dollars. But there's simply this good feeling that comes with helping people, especially the rough and gruff ones, the ones most people treat like door-to-door salespeople or over-zealous messengers.

Maybe the "God bless, man!" thing wasn't just this guy's hope for us, post-good deed. Perhaps it was a present thing in mine and Josh's lives. We were blessed right where we woke up. We were blessed the moment we made an offer on this little house of ours. I was blessed when I had to stay by myself for the first time. And we were blessed each day we opened the door for whoever ended up in our front yard.

Here again, Josh and I aren't building countless orphanages or overturning Roe v Wade. This isn't the stuff big Christian magazine reporters will beat down our door to get. God just has this way of making availability enough, especially when we are by ourselves in a new house with no one else to focus on. If you do nothing more than wake up, have the courage to open your door, and see who's out there, by yourself or not, and whether folks are screaming to call 9-1-1 or not, God has this solid way of taking care of the rest.

When we continuously label Monday as momentless, when we drive up to our dingy home and shake our heads, as if it's not enough, when we assume loneliness is a reason to lock our doors tight, we shut the door in God's face. That's not always the smartest thing to do. Once you take every little piece of every little day as an opportunity -- not necessarily to save the world, but to simply be right where you are -- stuff that matters starts to happen. You forget about the extra paperwork that comes with Monday. You forget about the leaky pipe in your guest bathroom that refuses to fix itself. You forget that you're by yourself, and you start remembering why you're here in the first place.

Live on the corner. Crane your neck around outside your front door. Wake up. Be present. Be by yourself, if you must. Put yourself in the most basic positions, in the most ordinary places, even if they're uncomfortable, and let God bless you, (wo)man!

# Church Games

My Taboo Thoughts and Mental Rituals OCD comes from some serious religious betrayal that I didn't always recognize as betrayal. After all, nobody was drinking Kool-Aid® and practicing polygamy, so I thought I simply mislabeled what was normal and healthy. Once I understood that I was a victim of spiritual abuse, I fumbled for words to express something that had been bottled up and was spewing over. Eventually, I was hurt and angry enough to pop the top and spew the truth myself: Some people don't mind manipulating the Gospel, standing behind a pulpit with their own mantra, and leading hundreds of others into hypnotizing, "justified" oblivion.

Behind all the anger, I was left confused, wondering if any part of my relationship with God could ever have been real, while I was bound by countless shackles that were portrayed as God's impossible, but somehow achievable, standards. In short, I was taught to serve the rules out of fear, not to serve God out of love. I learned to be so scared of doing the wrong thing that I missed so many opportunities to do the right thing. I was a robot switched on by man, not a worshipper empowered by the Holy Spirit.

By the time I turned 16, I realized the shepherd of my church herded sheep who only listened to him, rather than listening to the Holy Spirit. This shepherd said very little that lined up with the Bible, but as long as the women sheep wore long dresses and the men sheep wore a suit and tie like his, he used his rod to guide his wooly followers wherever he wanted them to go.

He could tell you that you couldn't approach Jesus; you had to wait for a "slap you off your seat" moment before God would count your repentance.

21

This shepherd could tell a girl she was a "whore," (yes, he said the actual word behind the pulpit), for wearing a short skirt to church, and shame her into believing that God expects us to be squeaky clean before we come to Him.

I had an honest talk with my mom, and she really listened to my fears and deep concerns about this place. Praise Jesus, our family made the decision to leave that church and attend another one, of the same Baptist denomination, with a more healed, approachable definition of God. This church gave women a little more freedom, the space to serve, the room to speak what God was saying to them, and we were allowed to wear blue jeans, sport black fingernail polish, and carry an ESV Bible, all at the same time.

Since I went to college in my hometown, I had the opportunity to continue serving in this church in my late teens and early twenties. I became the pianist for Sunday worship, as well as a youth group leader. As with most leadership roles, there came heavy responsibility, and there also came heavy-hitting haters. Unfortunately, the church tends to breed judgers, nitpickers, and gossips. Meanwhile, it's easy for the leaders and regular attendees of the church to blend their personal wants with Jesus' actual message. It becomes easy to unknowingly twist the truth when church members deem you "worthy" of serving as a leader. Therefore, sin or not, you tend to justify every decision you make, pushing your pedestal further into the stark stage lights-- regardless of knocking someone else out of the way.

It didn't take long for me to realize that lots of people, men in particular, had a hard time accepting that a single woman could lead. Do I think they even realized it? Absolutely not. I can't go on a total hate rant without admitting that they understood God's grace and kindness far more than I did. At the same time, it didn't mean they left me feeling great about myself when I walked out of the church doors by myself, got in my own car, and drove back to my parents' house. People talk. I knew that certain men had made comments about certain outfits that I dared to wear on the stage. Meanwhile, other men and women in the congregation wondered aloud how I had made it 22 years without getting married.

How had this new church, a shelter from the terrors of my former church, shamed my singlehood? How could I heal from their words, from their questions, especially when the hurt was unintentional?

But then I recall Photine, the woman at the well. She was the first one to whom Jesus publicly revealed Himself when He came to earth. She was an adulteress, an outcast, the one everyone labeled "not good enough." Yet, she was enough to be the first person chosen to learn the best secret ever. And Jesus was so moved by His mother Mary's belief that He answered her request with His first earthly miracle and turned water into wine. By the way, lots of scholars think Joseph was already dead at this point, making Mary a single woman. And the woman with the blood disorder, the woman that men trampled over in the street, barely brushed the hem of His garment and my Jesus put the whole world on pause to heal her. Jesus doesn't silence the lonely woman. Rather, He empowers her with His presence.

Let me say that one more time: Jesus doesn't silence the lonely woman; He empowers her with His presence.

Jesus doesn't use church to play wily games of matchmaker, assuming a woman's only spiritual goal is to be yoked to a man. Instead, He uses His presence to detangle a lonely heart of emptiness that comes from being suffocated by all the wrong things. Unfortunately, church culture has blurred that truth. I've heard countless people say that the best place to find your future spouse is at church, as if that's the bone dangled in front of the dog, the "treat" that serves as the only way to get us to church. But let me tell you this: You go to church to commune with God. Trust me, I met my first boyfriend at church. This tall, buff guy strolled in and sat one row in front of me. He was a total dream, the official husband package, until I dated him and he turned out to be a dud dude who was more concerned about investing in his next tattoo than working with Jesus to pull the weeds from his heart.

I didn't realize this culture-curated mirage at first. I thought my reward for showing up to church, serving in the church, would be to find a husband. Now, it seems pathetic, but it seems heartbreaking too. What I didn't realize then was that I had redefined church, much like the folks did at the previous church where I was exposed to such traumas. I twisted the meaning behind worship to fit my narrative, and it was a narrative that abused the strong role God gave to me as a woman. It was a narrative that left me splurging on outfits, buying a new (*and* appropriate) one every weekend to wear onstage, as long as the young, college baseball coach was attending service. The narrative left me going on youth trips to the beach and hoping I'd bump into a surfer whose faith was as solid as his wave skills. Forget ministering to the kids, right?

I made Jesus what I wanted Him to be; I made Him the avenue to finding a man. And that's the place where I lost control of my emotions, lost sight of Who God was. That's the exact place where I grew angry, even bitter, at serving in the church. And it was ALL my fault.

Now, I'll tell you, service in the church was hard work, even when my heart was in the right place. Church could be a vicious and dramatic place, making me focus on the heavenly reward instead of the earthly reaping. Meanwhile, I was expected to play the piano at these people's weddings and funerals and to carry the weight of pre-ceremony jitters and lost loved ones, a weight that was never mine to bear. It was a blessing when I could see this as the chance to serve, but when a woman is wheeling and dealing church to her advantage, and she rolls the love dice wrong, it becomes a curse.

Eventually, I snapped.

One morning, I was onstage preparing my music for the church service. People were already filing into their seats so I was in a hurry to get my stuff together. "When are you ever going to get married?" I heard one of the musicians ask, even though I wasn't talking to the guy. This conversation, this theme, came out of some conversation he must've had with himself. I turned in his direction, cocked my head, offered a sarcastic comment, and stormed off the stage.

How dare he ask me that, and right before church? Why would he ask that out of nowhere? It's not everyone's goal to get married by 19, but it was my dream, even if I didn't want everyone to know I was that desperate. I thought I was ready to get married at 19, and when that crashed and burned, I made it my mission to find the love of my life at church. Church had become a game, and again, it was all my fault. I didn't have any rules about the King James Bible, but I played my own church game, using pawns and moving youth members around until I could bump into a guy. I rallied band musicians and singers behind me, roping them into the obligation of bringing attractive male loved ones to church so I could casually meet them.

It was sick and so very LAME.

Unbeknownst to me, I had taken the one place that was meant to offer peace and had thrown it in a pile with the rest of my distracting loneliness. Church was coupled with not having a boyfriend. Thanks to lots of congregation members, it was a constant reminder that I was single. And thanks to one man's side comment about my "inappropriate" clothes, which made the church put a black curtain around the piano, I thought maybe I was a skank. I probably didn't deserve a boyfriend anyway. Perhaps, loneliness was my reward.

After I graduated college, I wasn't sure I wanted to continue serving in the church. I was tired, mainly tired of being single. In my irrational, immature head, that was the perfect reason to bow out. But deep down, the reason I walked away was because the dud dude with the tattoos came back into my life, ripped my heart out again, and I was too embarrassed to show my face in front of his family a second time. No one wants to be the good church girl who can't keep a guy. I let my perception of life, love, and loneliness steer me from serving. Looking back, now that I'm happily married to Josh, do I still think it was my time to leave? Absolutely. It was time to go, but I left a legacy of the lonely piano player who played all the games for all the wrong reasons.

As I reflect on my church experiences, it's no surprise that I've yet to find a healthy place to worship. Now that I'm grown and married, I made my own decision to never be part of a Baptist church again. That's not because I don't love and appreciate their beliefs, but my first experience in a Baptist church that had scary rules, and even scarier enforcement of those rules, was traumatizing. It was disturbing to the extent that I hold my breath when I see a church that looks similar to that one. If it's laden with a certain shade of brick, iron rails, and a corny sign with a church saying, I freak out. It's sad, but I've also traumatized myself. Even though I'm married now, and Mission Find A Husband is complete, how will I ever be sure that I'm serving for the right reasons?

I can't hide from the pew, though, and pretend that God won't ask me to step up. After all, He asks us to love and serve constantly. I've realized that my role is a little bigger now. It means something deeper than playing games. So, the next time someone nudges me behind a piano or microphone, it won't be about me and what I have to win. It'll be the opposite of manipulation, the opposite of what I grew to hate in church rules and in myself. Serving won't come from a place of anger or bitterness or manipulation because I won't look for things to go my way.

I'm not saying I won't get something out of it, but it'll be something that's less tangible and much better for my soul. It'll be something that won't leave me mad at the world or disappointed with who I am. If there's one thing I knew all along, but never admitted while serving in church, it's that I always have lots of my own issues to let Jesus help me sort and trash. If I'm serving from a place of humility, a place where I can accept that I'm serving because God calls really unqualified people, then my approach will be different.

It won't be a game of chance where I'm just hoping my spinner lands on the right number. There will be no whammies, no "go to jail" cards. I'm sure there will be more times when I feel like a loser, like someone who can't seem to get this faith thing right all the time. But there's grace that never existed before. It's a grace God gives when we step out of the way and let Him do things for His right reasons and in His right time.

\*\*\*

I can't imagine the physical pain Jesus endured on the cross. The agony is something that my brain rarely lets me ponder, let alone process. My understanding of the excruciating nightmare He went through makes me adore Him even more. But between the gruesome weight of the physical, mixed with the horrific burden of the spiritual, I think it's easy for us to neglect, even fail to realize, the emotional pain He endured and conquered on our behalf.

I'm not sure what your Sunday School days looked like, but around Easter, our class often walked through the Resurrection eggs. The teacher popped open each little egg. Some held a thorn for the crown of thorns, some had a nail representing the scars on His hands and feet, some had a little strip of cloth as a symbol of His burial clothes, and so on. The last egg was always empty, representing the powerful reminder that Jesus defeated death and saved us from our sins. Yet, there were so many other things Jesus suffered, had to bear, and conquered for us, simply because He loved us enough to protect us from their eternal harm.

I believe, when Jesus asked God, "Eloi, Eloi lama sabachthani?" ("My God, My God, why hast Thou forsaken me?"), He wasn't alone. I don't think God, being the good Father He is, turned His back on His Son. Jesus undoubtedly had the weight of sin on His battered, beautiful shoulders, but when did God not have the power to stare sin down and rip it apart for the sake of His Son?

Instead, I think Jesus might have chosen to hang on a lonely cross to defeat loneliness for us. God never designed us to be lonely. In fact, that's why God came to the Garden every day and walked and talked with Adam and Eve. He revels in His relationship with God the Son and God the Holy Spirit. He loved relationships then, and He still does.

God loves that connection so much that when Jesus died, He endured the trauma of feeling separated from His Father for the first time. He chose to feel separated, so one day, you and I would be free of loneliness too. He hates loneliness, despises the way it creeps into our lives and whisks our souls into a frenzy. He hates loneliness as much as He hates sin, so I am a total believer that He willingly conquered the ache and agony of isolation on the cross too.

If you're like I was a few years ago, before I realized Jesus' humble humanity, you might wonder if God gets some sick kick out of your loneliness. You might question if He enjoys watching you go on a date with a guy who makes you escape to the bathroom, text your mom, and beg her to come get you. I'll save you some time and promise that He doesn't work that way. If you think He enjoys watching men lie, cheat, and leave, just know that He endures the betrayal and loneliness you feel too.

I'll never forget the first time I found out my first love dud dude was balancing me and another girl at the same time. It crushed me. My heart was in so many pieces that there weren't enough hours in the night to even sweep up the shards. I was alone at my house one Friday evening. Everyone else had weekend plans, and after a hard run at the gym, I just wanted to come home and do nothing but stop thinking. I plopped on the floor, just me and dim light in the living room. My arms and legs shook, maybe from the workout, probably from the emotional exhaustion. I sprawled face down on the hardwood floor, and then I sobbed.

It was one of those guttural sobs that made me want to throw up and pop an

800 mg ibuprofen at the same time. But somewhere in the middle of that breakdown, Jesus picked me up and gave me back the pieces of my heart that I needed. He also kept the pieces that no longer served a purpose. Then day by day, He went behind the scenes and turned the shards into a story of loneliness restored.

I didn't find Mr. Right for several more years, but I felt Jesus with me, felt Him carrying me when I didn't want to feel anything, when I was too scared to let anyone else carry me. Truth be told, to this day, even though I'm now happily married, my heart still shatters and Jesus still picks up the shards. At the end of each day, though, He's always the One I choose to carry me through the night.

He remembers that He endured that exact pain so one day you'd be free of it too. Dear girl, He'll never leave you lonely. Have faith that God is too good to leave you without a mate:

> *Seek and read from the book of the LORD: Not one of these shall be missing; none shall be without her mate. For the mouth of the LORD has commanded, and his Spirit has gathered them.* Isaiah 34:16

God is selfless so He can be selfish for you. He's the kind of Father Who wants to spoil you with what you want, and then some. I'm not saying God will hand you a Ken. I mean, I truly prayed that God would give me a man with eight-pack abs and He handed me Josh Garland who only had a six-pack. But seriously, God gave me a man who was good for my soul, who would be there for me in ways that I'd never been there for myself. And yeah, it will all be in God's time, which is one of those clichés you don't want to hear, but it's true. It also is true that God is jealous for you and fighting to give you what your heart needs. He's too good to dangle dreams and hopes in your face, then snatch them away and use them like puppets of fear. And all along, it's His heart that will forever fulfill your longings.

Don't count out His goodness. Don't count out His love. And don't let anyone behind a pulpit, at your dinner table, or hiding behind a text message, ever tell you otherwise.

# Welcome the Unknown

Old hymns remind me of the church I grew up in, so it's hard to enjoy them. I can feel the suspension of chords on the piano, the awkward waaaaaa-ing of the organ, and suddenly, it's hard to hang onto the words. Panic doesn't leave any room for healthy lyrical concentration, particularly when you're sitting in a church that thrives in making you feel like you're headed to hell, or a church that lets the music ladies wear dresses with awkward, distracting shoulder pads.

It took a while, but I eventually realized that in addition to the most traditional, well-known hymns like *Amazing Grace* and *Victory in Jesus*, standard Christian messages and catchphrases freak me out. It sounds pathetic and seems odd, but if you've never been deeply wounded by a church, I highly encourage you to find a friend who has and talk with them. Get to know people who are wary of church, and don't assume that they are wary of Jesus. Don't condemn them. Try not to make weird faces when they say that *Amazing Grace* incites an anxiety attack. Just listen. That's what Jesus does.

A church saying that freaks me out most is: "Jesus left the 99 for you." Don't get me wrong: I'm totally thankful He left everyone else just to hunt me down. You'll never hear me argue the truth behind this phrase, but what puts me on edge is that the church rarely addresses the flip side of the story. Yes, while the one sheep that went astray did lots of dumb things, it still made the right decision in the end and came safely back into the flock. There's just an awkward, uneasy feeling for me when nobody addresses the humanity of the other 99 sheep. Did they feel abandoned and alone? Were they frustrated? Did it seem to them that the Shepherd left them for days on end, without food and water and facing the scariness of the night? Was Jesus okay with how they felt? Or were they bad, selfish sheep? Or worse, were they even sheep? Or just wolves in sheep's clothing?

Without a doubt, Jesus is omnipresent and doesn't need any of my, nor any sheep's, help to be present everywhere. He always has, and always will, hunt down the lost sheep while forever being with the other 99, even when they're too ignorant to see it. I'll never challenge that beautiful characteristic of the Godhead. I recognize, too, that it's easy for Christians to feel alone. It's not that this is caused by Jesus. It's just that this world has a way of draining us and convincing us that we aren't worth anyone staying with us.

When the church fails to bring up the other characters in the story, when church leaders don't feel the need to wrestle hard questions in front of others, I'm always afraid that a plotline is missing, or worse, that I'm wrong for even questioning things. Good, healthy, stable Christians don't think this way, right? Thus, I'm inducing the fear that I'm a hell-bound sinner who is forever punished for asking what I think is the hard stuff, but it doesn't seem hard for the "good" Christians. What I'm slowly learning, though, is that it's okay to have countless questions, the kind of questions for which humans don't have the answers. And I sometimes wonder if that's why you never hear about the 99 sheep. Maybe church leaders are afraid they'll say something wrong, or mess something up when they talk about a new topic that they can't directly reference anywhere in Scripture. Maybe it's hard to talk about a topic and absolutely have to go with the Holy Spirit's conviction and nothing else.

As a perfectionist and traumatized church-goer, I understand how scary it can be to bear both right and wrong, especially in a leadership role. It's even more frightening when you're leading others regarding a topic you don't feel qualified to address. You feel, if you don't say anything, then you'll leave the rest of us knowing nothing. While Jesus understands that we'll never have all of the answers, I don't think He's content with us never asking Him hard questions and never walking through confusing conversations with others.

That's how you find your soulmate, right? Sure, you don't spring 20 questions on them on day one, but once you realize there's something extra special about the guy, you want to know more. You want to know the grittier, intense details. For me, I started poking and prodding Josh about church and his relationship with Jesus about a month after we started dating, because it was and is that important to me. I started asking about his salvation story, his journey with God. I wanted all the answers with all the background info. Even if it was what I didn't want to hear, I demanded the truth.

Of course, he could've played a church game, saying all the right things and showing up just because that's what I wanted him to do. We could've called it fair, but I wanted to know Josh's heart. That meant I had to ask personal questions, even the kind that felt awkward rolling off my tongue, the kind that made me cringe when I asked them. I had to question why I had to ask him to come to church, and had to ask questions like why he seemed to have a bitter taste in his mouth when it came to church. Not that we didn't have some fantastic, encouraging conversations about this stuff, but when you're taught to follow only one narrative and not to see all sides of everyone else's story, you keep quiet. You never fully connect to other people, or worse, you make assumptions, judge people, and you are the exact opposite of what you're supposed to be. Working this way, you don't realize that the church wronged your boyfriend just as badly as it wronged you. You miss opportunities to better understand God's grace, which always paves the way for you to extend His grace to others.

While Josh was in Indiana, Florida, and anywhere else the sky took him, my toughest question was why my dreams had been put on hold for the sake of his. Sure, we'd both been wronged by the church, but I was the one who stayed faithful the whole time. I was the one who kept going to church, a Baptist church, the one that honored all the rules and never bucked the system. I was the one who worked so hard to make sure my education was paid for and my career all set. I was the one who did everything right. Meanwhile, Josh grew bitter and left the church; he left the steeple for nearly a decade. So, with this blatant abandonment, why was he closing in on his dream to fly an airplane? Why was my dream to have a book published out of reach? Better yet, why was he getting a dream that tortured me?

Why did God want me to feel like I was second fiddle to an airplane? Why was God so okay with Josh chasing down his flight hours, while I was chased down by intrusive thoughts and cornered in my lonely, dark bedroom? I was told Jesus would never leave or forsake me, but it was hard to feel that. It's one thing to accept the truth, but it's another to feel it deep in your bones.

31

And honestly, that's all I had become-- dry, lifeless bones.

In my whole life, everyone around me seemed fixed by the church sayings, like when the pastor said Christians are never alone, everyone else there instantly felt surrounded by peace and people. Why was I so different? What bad thing had I done so I could never feel like a normal Christian?

What I didn't realize was, it's so easy for people to worship a pastor, to get so wrapped up in what the church is saying, what the church is doing. It's so easy to get wrapped up in those ways that we follow the person, the building, to satisfy our souls. It's easy to join the head bobbing and amen-ing when everyone else is doing it, but that leaves so much room for a disconnect as soon as you leave the church parking lot.

So maybe God is answering my question here. Maybe the 99 do feel abandoned and confused sometimes, so they seek refuge in all the wrong places that are really good at looking like the right places. We wear the church sweatshirt, we show up to the Wednesday night fun night, we repeat all the churchy sayings as means to belong and feel secure. Maybe the reason the preachers so often preach about the one sheep is that although that sheep is caught somewhere in sin, it's meeting the character of Jesus head-on. It doesn't need all the other sheep that are trapped in the gate to tell it how to live. They all have the same viewpoint, same perspective, but the one stray sheep sees Jesus getting things done, doing things in His holy, selfless way.

I try not to beat myself up about how awkward I feel around the idea of church, even though I'll forever attend out of an honest mixture of religious OCD that makes me feel obligated, and the beautiful prodding of the Holy Spirit. Maybe I'm saying this to make myself feel better, but perhaps I'm the one sheep that's already been found and I'm still enroute to the fold. I see Jesus for how lovely He is, and I'm His, but I also see the 99 sheep struggling, feeling abandoned, and unintentionally bucking the nature of God, all for the sake of assuring themselves they still count, that they're still sheep.

That prayer I've learned to whisper when I'm really confused, when my OCD is raging, when I have questions that the church never seemed to want me to ask, is, "God, just stay." I can almost see me thrown over Jesus' shoulders, covered in mangy wool with stubby feet. I can see the fold, see all the sheep safe there, but I don't know how I feel about being around those sheep. I'm not sure I measure up to their whiteness. I'm not sure I want to measure up to their whiteness that might come from a place of wanting to belong, not from a place of taking Jesus on His Word.

I don't think Jesus would be too quiet on a trip like this. He's probably telling me that everything's okay, that I'll always have a place to serve in the fold, but I know me. I'm a sheep that would not only be dumb but would also be scared. I've seen too many wolves, fought too many coyotes, to think that it's as easy as Jesus leading me in and locking me up tight in His fold forever. Likewise, I don't think I would be too quiet on a trip like this, but I imagine I'd be saying the same thing, praying the same prayer, over and over: "God, just stay."

Truth is, I don't need the other 99 sheep to feel safe and to feel like I belong. I need a Savior Who isn't afraid when I take off running in a different direction, when I ask questions that have me standing on the outside looking in, when I seem like a total church hater who is more scared than spiteful.

It's bittersweet when Jesus answers certain questions. Most of the time, you either get the exact answer you wanted, or you get an answer that calls you to step up. So, when the opportunity arose to share this book, to be traditionally published, I had to face the reality that I had realized my dream before Josh realized his. Becoming a Delta pilot is his dream, it is not being a flight instructor, and while a global pandemic put his dream on hold, it catalyzed mine. A pandemic that has shaken my very core is what God used to answer my questions and fulfill my dreams. I have weird feelings; I'm feeling ecstatic for myself, but incredibly sad for Josh. I'm proud of myself for writing a book, but I feel guilty for how I've treated Josh.

Despite it being a dream, having this book published hasn't fulfilled me. I don't feel like I've reached a place of arrival, or that I could die right now and be content. It's not that I'm not thankful for this incredible opportunity, but it is truly Jesus who validates my life. I've tried to think of a not-so-churchy way to say this, but Jesus really is the only One Who satisfies our hearts. Nothing else will do that, no matter how many times you volunteer for a church function, nor how many Sunday School classes you attend.

It's just Jesus. It's just Jesus and you, the dumb, wandering, lonely sheep, so why should the other 99 grab the headlines anyway?

I'm trying to say, go ahead and ask the questions. Don't avoid them. Jesus wants to teach a student who's inquisitive, who knows that the Teacher is so kind, so selfless, that He will use the questions to better answer Who He is.

There's something about recognizing God in all aspects of life that makes His presence so much louder, so much more visual. We can't technically hear or see God, but these questions take my senses to a spiritual level. I think that's what the Bible means when it refers to being quickened by the Spirit. All of a sudden, the two-dimensional things of this world fade out and God's surrounding, three-dimensional movements are so in your face that you can't deny them.

God has had humanity's best interest at heart since day one, even though you can't put a time label on God's omniscience. He and Jesus created this plan to bail you out of the nasty stuff in the end, but first They want your heart ready for the rescue. They want you to realize that training the soul to ask questions for the sake of eternity is the heart of success.

Trust me, there are days when I don't want awkward questions and loneliness to be my story, even when that seems like the passageway to a dream of having this book published. When I need to ask the questions and wait for the answers, when I'm feeling mentally healthy and able to be strong, I can go back in my mind to that first church. That was the place where I fought wearing dresses and tights, where sermons were long and full of hellfire, but I can think of a few songs that crack the outer layers of my scarred, calloused heart and leave room for healing, not trauma:

> Oh, to grace how great a debtor
> Daily I'm constrained to be
> Let that goodness like a fetter
> Bind my wandering heart to Thee
> Prone to wander, Lord, I feel it
> Prone to leave the God I love
> Here's my heart, oh, take and seal it Seal it for Thy courts above
> Here's my heart, oh, take and seal it
> Seal it for Thy courts above
> *Come Thou Fount*

# A Grand Canyon

I'm not sure how strict your parents were, but mine never had to rein me in. There were no late-night curfews or cellphone stipulations. I was never grounded nor told I couldn't go to a birthday party or a school function. The lack of those parental restrictions was because I disciplined myself. I was my own parent, teacher, and judge. Mom has said I put myself in timeout or sent myself to my room when I thought I had done something wrong.

Do I remember doing this as a child? Not particularly. Do I remember putting myself in my room as a teenager, convulsing from sobs and self-hate, when I accidentally tapped the back of Mom's car with my Chevy? You bet. Even as a "mature" adult, I send myself to my room to have an angry meltdown when I think I've messed up. I don't let Josh in the room to check on me, either. In my mind, the guilty one doesn't deserve condolences or a pat on the back.

Even though my parents always trusted me to do the right thing, it was surprising when they let me visit Josh out west about five months after we started dating. That idea left room for some gray, risqué stuff, particularly when I mentioned Las Vegas. Who could blame them for pausing before saying yes? But we all knew, at the end of the day, that having premarital sex would be my doom, especially when I pitched a fit with Josh about having my own bed. So, there was no way sex was going to happen.

Josh had taken a month-long road trip to visit all the major sites across the northern border and down the west coast of the country; it was his own celebration of freedom before finishing his degree and starting a job, which

35

would never include taking a month off. I flew out to meet him in Las Vegas. We walked through all the casinos and tried not to die from 116-degree weather. After a day there, we routed a trip to the Grand Canyon.

It's definitely a God spot, maybe even God's footprint on earth. What's so beautiful and overwhelming about the place is that you can't find the end of it. The Canyon stretches so far out that you wonder why you can't see it from your backyard-- no matter which state you live in. In theory, I should be able to sip my sweet tea on the back porch and toss mounds of red Georgia clay into its mouth.

There were plenty of touristy things to do when we got to the Canyon. There was a gift shop full of standard post cards and pens to send back home. There was a snack kiosk where we could renourish our bodies that were having total meltdowns from the oven-like desert heat. (It beats me why they put the snack station at the front entrance before the adventure began, rather than closer to the hiking spots.) Among the many things to do was riding the shuttle that carted guests to each major site or visiting the glass bridge and walking across the transparent path. There, you could see the bottom of the Canyon right under your feet. They even had donkey tours available to ride a switchback trail into the Canyon's camping site.

But since Josh and I had never been basic tourists, and since someone had not too long before fallen off their donkey and died, we opted out of the basic options. At the time, I was a little obsessed with my purple Fitbit and the step track feature, so we decided to walk to each site rather than take the sissy option and trolley around. If we were hiking the Canyon, then I was getting my 10,000 steps.

Walking the less popular sites meant fewer people. It was still a blaring scorcher of a day, but there was something refreshing and peaceful about the abyss of purple and brown canyons that weren't suffocated by people taking pictures. Those canyons reminded me that we must be pretty special. After all, the God of everything, Who spoke all of this into existence, still chose to send His Son to die and rise again for us. On the flip side, there was also a special kind of peace that I had to have with Jesus when Josh convinced me to walk out on one of the Canyon's rocky ledges without a harness or guardrails to keep me planted. That was the kind of Jesus peace that meant I was cool with the increasing possibility of death.

Now, the world is full of danger junkies who skydive, cliff dive, belay up mountains, tank dive with sharks, etc. They are some crazies and I'm a little jealous of them, but most of us don't prefer to face death, not when death uses our biggest fears as easy manipulation tactics.

Spiders freak me out, I admit. Nothing should need that many little pointy legs to walk. Still, I can hold my breath and keep my heart rate calm enough to grab a broom or paper towel and kill one. I don't like clowns. I don't like anything using blue face paint and a red squeaky nose to hide its true colors. That didn't stop me from taking a selfie with one of those weirdos at a ridiculous "haunted" farm in Alabama, though. But heights? Heights are a different story.

Unfortunately, there's no sucking it up or taking a selfie with heights. My heart rate won't go down, and even if I could take a broom and whack heights in the face, I'd be too scared to walk to the broom closet.

Honestly, I don't know where this fear comes from, nor do I understand its core. For most people, the fear of falling from a height is what scares them. Sure, that's a chunk of the uneasiness I feel when I'm creaking and making my way up to the top of a roller coaster, but I feel like there's something else about being so high in the sky that makes me nervous. After all, I still use the "I'm scared of heights" thing when I fly, but I can't magically fall out of an airplane when there's this nice, unkempt blue carpet under my feet. So, what is it about heights that lurches my stomach?

I feel like there's no control, and that might be where the fear originated. I have nothing that I can bank on to keep me cinched to the ground, even if I do have something to keep me cinched to the ground. Rationale goes out the window when heights are an issue, so even when there's a guardrail to keep me safe, I'm still convinced I can't get too close. It's as if I lose the ability to control my body and my brain.

Since the Grand Canyon is one of the Seven World Wonders, I figured I would be completely captivated by its beauty. No doubt, the Canyon's a stunner, and the vastness will make your lungs forget how to pump air, but as soon as you feel like going off-road with it, the stubby bushes lining its layers look a little scarier and the pretty purple rocks aren't as fun to climb.

One of the Canyon's less traveled trails had this spearhead of jagged rock that shot out into open air. It was a giant rock, no doubt, but it had so many layers stacked on top of itself that there was barely room for my feet to fit on the outer edge. It was breathtakingly beautiful, but terrifying. This was no basic glass-bottom floor experience. There were no guardrails there, either. There was no nothing but open air. Of course, Josh wanted to walk out on this little spot to get a "grand" view of the Grand Canyon, but it looked grand right where I was, which was far, far away from the suspended rock. Naturally, since we were dating and still in that phase of constantly trying to remain impressive, I side-stepped my way out onto the rock, but only long enough to take a necessary picture before heading back to safety.

I didn't shake that fear for the rest of the day. I had faced my fear of heights but was still stuck in adrenaline mode. It's funny, but I began by planning a great adventure that would be one for the books. Instead, I fell back into the car exhausted, sunburnt, and weary from a scarring experience. While going to the Grand Canyon was a decent thing to brag about, I was petrified half of the time, afraid to get the full view, for fear of my feet losing their grip on the ground.

At the same time, there was a beauty to the weariness, even when the fear that made me scared seemed to keep me from something fun. Oftentimes, we don't prefer weariness because we live in a culture that only prefers the pretty picture in front of the Grand Canyon that has to be posted as soon as we find cell service again. Meanwhile, that same culture abuses the cycle of schedules, making us weary slaves to the social media post, to the job, to the side gig, to the soccer team. We have defined weariness as defeat with a side of premature crow's feet that probably kept us from getting an extra ten "likes" on Instagram. Perhaps we should be weary in a different way:

> Isaiah 51:3 says, *But they who wait for The Lord shall renew their strength; they shall mount up with wings like eagles; they shall run and not be weary; they shall walk and not faint.*

If we're willing to face the first part of that verse, then weariness indeed has a place in our journey with Jesus. After all, if our strength needs to be renewed, that means we're tired, worn down, and need a break. Meanwhile, church leaders and church-y memes often romanticize the waiting to a Christian. It's supposed to be the time when the seed sprouts into a full-bloomed flower, or when the knight in shining armor finally bumps into us at the coffee shop and asks for our phone number and doesn't forget about us two days later. The church has taught us to obsess over the final result of the waiting, rather than embracing the humanity, and even the agony, of the weary process.

***

Agonizing is probably one of the best ways to describe how I felt when Josh was gone. Having a mental disorder that thrives on quietness is no fun when the quietness never ends. It took everything in me to have the nerve to steady my hands, get up off the couch, and tell my brain to shut up so I could feed myself. Often, I drifted so far into numbness that I would neglect the barest form of self-care. I wouldn't eat, wouldn't really sleep, wouldn't force myself to go for walks or meet a friend at the gym, all because my fear had worn me out.

I wasn't really scared that someone was going to break into the house while Josh was gone. Yeah, the basement was creepy from time to time, but there were much bigger issues in front of me. I wasn't scared that I would suddenly forget how to check the mail, start a fire in the fireplace, or take out the trash. What I was terrified of was the weariness. Much like the total, lockdown-type fear I had while tiptoeing to the ledge of the Grand Canyon, fighting the fear was too much for me. I wasn't a pretty flower. My knight in shining armor was stuck thousands of feet in the sky, several states away, unable to ride across the countryside and save my day. Waiting wasn't getting me anywhere. Weariness didn't seem to be fulfilling any promises, either. I had that much right.

What weariness was doing was slowing me down, pulling me away from everything that had always made me feel level and planted. Weariness was putting me flat on my face. Being flat on my face, prostrated before Jesus, sounds like this poetic, angelic lesson in humility that has already been mastered: "Betwixt the pulpit and organ lieth Peyton, a humble servant, whose prostrate position exemplifies every bit of righteous understanding. She doth know what is honoring and proper in the eyes of The Lord."

But being face down, pinned to the ground by fear or weariness, or maybe both, looks much crazier than that. Do you remember when Hannah was begging God for a son? When Eli found her in the church, he thought she was drunk. Her prayer was that wild. But it worked. God honored her crazy prayer by giving her Samuel, a child who grew into the prophet we know as the guy in charge of calling David out as God's anointed king of Israel. Cool, huh?

Remember the lady with the blood disorder that I mentioned earlier? She touched the hem of Jesus' garment, which means she was probably belly crawling her way between stinky feet on the dusty earth, just to get near Him. Her prayer and her faith were nasty in the rawest form. But notice that the wild, gritty prayers are the ones that get answered. They are the prayers that come from a place of fear and weariness. They come from hopelessness that knows only to cling to the hope of the One so unlike the rest of us.

Waiting isn't meant to make us a pretty flower or land us the perfect husband. Waiting is meant to wear us down, to make us so low that Jesus' bloom is the only One we pluck. Jesus is the only One we have to stay up and talk with, for hours and hours on end.

Rather than running from waiting, rather than running from fear, perhaps we're meant to be awestruck by the weariness. Maybe there is a wonder that grows from the weariness and carries the soul much further than merely across a Grand Canyon. Maybe our weariness carries us from room to room, from the bathroom floor to the living room floor, from the corner of the kitchen to the carpet by our bedside, where we crave His hope more than we crave the endgame of our weary waiting.

Might not sound fun, but when you realize the agony of having no one else to turn to, a dusty, stinky, earthen floor is the gateway to God.

***

In only five days, I have a really important doctor's appointment; it's the kind of appointment that will ensure I don't have cancer. I get funny looks from people when I explain my medical history, but that makes sense. Most people in their mid-twenties don't feel the threat of the c-word, but its reality smacked me square in the face when I turned 21.

I went to my ob-gyn for my annual checkup, no big deal, but a few weeks after the appointment, I got a phone call that the cells on my cervix were abnormal. This wasn't an "Oh, whatever," abnormal; this was a, "You need to get back in the office because there could be a problem," abnormal. Fast forward five years later and I'm still battling these funky, precancerous cells. Thanks to a good, good God, I've yet to have cancer, but I have had a piece of my cervix removed to avoid some nasty cells developing into cervical cancer.

I had to have my cells examined every three months last year, and all of those results came back normal, Praise the Lord! But while I've dodged the bullet, I'm still gun shy about saying I'm a totally healthy young lady, and that's all thanks to the waiting.

Since everything has seemed fine after they removed a piece of my cervix, I haven't had to go back to the doctor for a full year. Do you know how many bad things can happen in a year, though? How many cells can have an identity crisis and turn on their own host? Do you know how many completely illogical, bad things a brain with OCD can invent in a year? I've lost track counting.

Waiting has wearied me. It has given fear space to push its agenda and script plenty of worst-case scenarios. Now, if I'm going to practice what I preach, I have to believe God is writing a story so much richer, so much more powerful than anything that fear and lies could scribble. If weariness and waiting are where I grow, then I'll sit with the unknown and call it a growing pain. I'll look at the scenarios and play out the hope that God provides. I'll probably cry, freak out, cry, and freak out again, waiting on these results.

But if I am sure God's favorite place to be is in the middle of my hurt, fear, and mess, then I choose to believe I can't be any place safer than I am right now. I'll be honest, I'm not in a mood to mount up with wings like eagles. Waiting has me tired, wanting to rest on the ground, so until I have some test results, I'll wait in the dirt. I'll sprawl on the floor, knowing God is the lifter of my head. He'll hold me up. He'll make sure my face is pointing toward heaven this time, not the floor. And He'll carry me through and through.

41

# Rocky the Chipmunk

I'm a hoarder. Granted, I don't stow away ten-year-old field day t-shirts or Beanie Baby collections, but I stash money and time whenever I can. If I don't have a gift card to my favorite boutique, I usually cry on the inside and wait until my birthday rolls around so I land the gift card jackpot or someone (Josh) feels guilty enough to load money onto an app. If I want a week of paid vacation to roll over to the next year, you bet I'll turn down long weekend getaways and Spring Break fun and take only two of my three weeks off. But only one month into Josh being gone, I woke up on a crisp Tuesday and knew I wouldn't make it into the office, not that day. My body, head to toe, ached with a brutal concoction of exhaustion mixed with whatever terrible weed blooms in Georgia throughout October. Every sinus cavity behind my face banged its drums, protesting my puny attempt to get out of bed.

Most days, I have a major hang-up with taking time for myself, even when I feel sick. This isn't only because I prefer to hoard time, but self-care is quite the antagonist in my world. Taking time for me, whether I'm wearing a blueberry acai mask or scrolling through Disney®, makes things quiet and still. Watching a movie might seem like the good kind of loud that drowns out life or anything else I'm avoiding, but it doesn't force my brain to focus. I don't do well with quiet, stillness, and a lack of focus.

OCD thrives off silent headspace; it is quite the strategic, cruel monster that way. When my brain is too settled, OCD will tiptoe to the back room of my frontal lobe where it's dark, but not dusty. Let's be honest, OCD visits this back room too often for cobwebs to settle. It will prance to the dingy, rusty filing cabinet in the corner of the room and locate the top drawer where all my biggest fears are. OCD moves quickly and knows how to jimmy the lock on this drawer. OCD closes its eyes, just for spite, and randomly selects one of my top fears to prey upon. When I'm lounging around in an acai mask, with no one around, OCD usually holds up a list of all the people I love but includes ways I could hurt them. I start thinking about whether the text I sent to Mom woke her up, which could make her a sleepy, unsafe driver. And what if she gets in a wreck and dies? Then, it's my fault.

I tried to watch *Oliver & Company* not too long ago, a wonderful 90s cartoon about unlikely animal friends, but OCD quickly reminded me of all the abused animals I can't rescue because I don't know where they are. But if I knew where they were, I'd rescue them. But shouldn't I feel guilty for not doing everything I can to find ways to find them and rescue them? Needless to say, I didn't make it five minutes into the movie without turning it off and forcing myself to only think about the two dogs that Josh and I have saved.

These are only minor, very minor, files that OCD pulls when I'm all alone in the quiet, especially when I'm trying to take care of myself. So, when I called in sick and stayed home from work, I wasn't sure what kind of "rest" I would actually get. As life goes, I had already agreed, at least, to work from home, answering emails and hopping on meetings when necessary, but I realized I didn't have my work computer. I threw on a ball cap, debated throwing on makeup, didn't throw on makeup, then the dogs and I bee-bopped to the office. I snatched up my computer and left before anyone could offer, "Oh, Peyton. You look tired. Everything okay?" Then I cruised back home.

As soon as I let Alfie and Daisy out of the backseat, they took off toward the front yard, which isn't their usual play place. The front yard is small, boring, and has lots of brick-like pinecones that are no fun to tread on. As soon as I recognized that both of them were attacking a drainpipe, it made sense. Our front yard had lots of little squirrels and chipmunks, and the little scraping noises and vibration of the drainpipe confirmed that one of those poor guys was staked out in a slippery, unsafe spot. Before I could get the dogs away from the metal pipe, the critter tried to escape, but he wasn't fast enough. Alfie picked up this precious little chipmunk and threw him in the air like one of his chew toys. With the hype of the chase over, Alfie and Daisy trotted away, unamused by the poor critter. I didn't have lots of time to think, so I

43

went sumo wrestler-mode quickly, barreling through the front yard, beating my dogs out of the path, and snatching up the terrified chipmunk.

Mom and Maw Maw have yet to understand why the chipmunk didn't eat my hand off. He didn't scratch, bite, fight, nothing. His little tummy was rising and falling way too fast for him to worry about who else was grabbing him. I wasn't sure if he was dying or in shock, but I tucked him into my comfy red sweatshirt and hovered over him like my dad hovered over me when I slid out of the birthing canal. "You're going to be just fine. You're safe now," I said over and over. And over and over again.

I bounced him up and down, up and down, toting him from room to room inside the house for what felt like forever, waiting to see if he would live or die. I called Mom and Maw Maw, drilling them with questions, hoping one of them would surprise me with some distinct chipmunk knowledge, but they both said to wait it out. I couldn't find any blood, nor mangled ligaments, but I had no idea whether his organs were mushed up or shot from the shock.

How he didn't drown from the number of tears I dumped on his head is a total God thing. Once I calmed down and realized he was going to make it, I found an old cardboard box and nestled him inside. Google® said to give him fruit, so I mashed some banana, added a fig to the menu, and spent one-million years outside finding the perfectly curved leaf to hold some water for him. After he ignored all of my provisions, I swaddled him in a sunflower dish towel and commenced Chipmunk Watch.

Before my motherly duties and security details were complete, I needed to give him a name. I assumed he was a boy based on no biological investigation, but strictly on my woodland animal ignorance, so I named him Rocky. After all, God made this little critter a fighter. He'd faced a pack of sausage ball dogs and a monsoon of Peyton's panicked tears and was still breathing. And I was banking on his fictional namesake prodding him to bust out of the sunflower dish towel, throw a leather-jacketed arm over the side of the box, and say, "Ay! Yo, Adrian!"

I'm not sure if you've ever rescued an animal, or ever stared at a really cute, cocooned chipmunk in a cardboard box, but you can't just look at it. You have to pick it up and cuddle it.

Naturally, Rocky didn't stay in his cardboard box for long because I scooped him up and nestled him in the crook of my arm while I answered emails and attended virtual meetings. His comfort level grew as he shimmied his way out of his little corner and rested his head on my laptop, the rest of his fuzzy body sprawled on my stomach. I'm not sure if he'd ever had any other close contact with humans, but he felt 100 percent safe; he trusted me.

Rocky and I hung out like this from about ten in the morning until around 2:30 in the afternoon. Maw Maw told me I should keep an eye on him for about four or five hours, then see how he did outside. I didn't realize it would break my heart to tote him outside and set him free, and I had a total meltdown. I took him to the front yard, close to several bushes where he could hide, and set him down on the grass and leaves. I told Rocky it was time to go back home, but he wouldn't move. Sure, we had been buddies because I saved his life, but I thought he would scamper away the moment he was back in his element. But he stayed still, near-motionless. Rocky wasn't budging.

I lost it. There's no telling what my neighbors thought of a girl sobbing her eyes out and yelling at a cardboard box to go someplace where it was safe. I didn't know if this was a sign that I should keep him, but how could I keep him as a pet when my dogs were the reason he almost died? I kept crying, telling Rocky to go back home. Eventually, he scampered toward the bushes. One hop, two hops, three hops, four hops-- gone. I walked the front yard for several minutes, turning over leaves and anything else to make sure he was out of harm's way.

For months, and I mean months, I checked the front yard for Rocky. Whether I was leaving for work, coming home from work, or checking out a pack of squirrels gang-banging through the neighborhood, I searched for him. I'd also back my car up and down the driveway, multiple times in one sitting, just to make sure I hadn't run over him. Sure, I saw several chipmunks scouting the perimeter, but none of them felt or looked like Rocky. He was abnormally small for a chipmunk, which meant he was either a baby or he wasn't a he. And when October turned into a much colder November and December, and even more icy, bitter January, I peeped outside and called for him, trying to see if he had found a little burrow where he could snuggle up and stay warm.

If you have OCD like me, and you can't let go of worries and deep emotions, and you have a panic attack trying to watch *Oliver & Company*, it should be no surprise that I googled Bible verses about God and animals and how He protects them. I wanted confirmation from God that He had his own SWAT team of angels ready to take out any fox, coyote, or vicious animal that would try to hurt Rocky. This is what I found in Psalm 50:11:

*I know all the birds of the hills, and all that moves in the field is mine.*

Rocky counts as "all that moves in the field," so I have no doubt that God is taking care of Rocky. Kid you not, I wrote that Bible verse on a sticky note and taped it to the top of my cubicle at work.

Since then, Josh and I have moved, downsizing from a three-bedroom house with a ridiculous monthly rent to a cozy one-bedroom apartment that we like much better than anticipated, so I don't get to talk to Rocky. I don't get to call for him, look for him, or double check that I haven't run over him in the driveway. The good part about my absence is, while I can't look out for him, I'm also not The Commander in Chief of legions of seven-headed angels. So, if God says everything that moves is His, then Rocky is well-taken care of. He's probably holed up in a 1,000-square foot burrow with velvet couches and a French press coffee flask, hosting evening parties featuring his story about the one time he survived two vicious sausage ball dogs and lived with a human who served him water on a leaf.

God brought Rocky into my life and out of my life in a matter of hours. Maybe it was so I could realize that I can't really hold onto anything. I can't hoard stuff. Time isn't in my control. The bad, scary OCD voices that creep up when I'm all by myself, trying to make sure I go insane, aren't in my control, either. That is a terrifying, but peaceful, relief all at once. And while I felt this deep pit in my stomach when I had to let Rocky go, the same kind of pit I felt when Josh packed up the Prius® and left for a new airport hours and hours away, God was showing me that my loneliness had meaning.

So many times, we want God's definition of "meaning" to reap earthly benefits for us. We want a reward at the end of the finish line that matches every dream we've ever tacked on a Pinterest board. But this meaning was deeper. It was the kind of meaning that reminded me, on really hard days, "Yeah, God really does have this whole thing under control." Just as I was yanking Rocky away from my dogs, thwarting danger, providing all the necessary nutrients and love, God had been doing the same things for me.

He knows how vicious loneliness is when you have OCD. He also knows that running away from it only makes it stronger. He knows that trying to take care of yourself can turn into a combustive catalyst for total meltdowns. He knows how exhausting and terrifying reality can be. At the same time, He knows just how good He is at wrapping us up in sunflower dish towels, giving us the good stuff that we usually want to ignore, and drowning us in His tears. All of that means something far greater than we will ever understand on this side of heaven.

If God has made it clear that everything that moves is His, then with every click of the remote, with every nose scrunch I make when my blueberry acai mask crinkles up, He's with me.

If He's with me in all of that lackadaisical nothingness, then He's with Rocky.

And you best bet He's with you too.

# Gentle Sparrow

I don't remember every single second about the day I received my Cherokee Native American name. Maybe because I was only five years old. Or was I six? Maybe because the whole campfire fiasco was too weird to process and retain. Who knows? What I remember most is a goldfish, some feathers, and a leathery-faced man stomping around in some dirt and worn-down grass, asking me the most ridiculous question I ever have been and ever will be asked.

The morning of the naming ceremony, Dad brought me to this big dirt pit and told me to stand by him. Other people I can't pair faces with stood in the worn grass alongside us, and together, we formed a big circle around this old, leathery guy sporting a big feather headdress and wearing a frown with layers of wrinkles. Leather Face took a few laps around us and divulged some special Native American secret stuff I don't remember, but after the secretive, yet generic details, things quickly got personal. He walked up to each person in the circle, got all in their bubble, asked them some really cool questions that I couldn't make out, then presented their Native American name to everyone else in the woodsy circle.

Everything seemed so secret agent-ish, so I was prepared for a question like, "Are you ready to tackle and tame a wolf?" or "Are you qualified to master the ways of the primitive bow and arrow?" You know, something Pocahontas could answer or sing in negative five seconds. Before I could come up with anything more intense that I might be asked, Leather Face slowly, and dramatically, came up to my dad and asked him some sort of secret question, then announced his name was Night Wolf, the protector of the family. He still likes to bring up this random cool fact about being the big, bad protector of the family when all of us girls gang up on him at the dinner table.

My father, now Night Wolf, meant I was obviously to be called Eye of the Tiger, Raven Claw, or something fierce. Right? There was just no way around a savage name now. Right?

"Do you like goldfish?" Leather Face asked me.

This was my top-secret question-- my preference, or lack thereof, for these little fish that live an average of two weeks.

"Yes," I answered, stuttered, choked out. I mean, was this a joke? Surely there was another question to follow, like, "Have you ever heard the legend of the Big Goldfish that, once caught, will enable your tribe to win all battles for generations to come?" Or maybe he was wanting to know if my Native American nature skills allowed me to communicate with goldfish. There were no more questions, though, so I had to answer this measly one with some form of honesty. I didn't dislike the fish. They had never altered my life in some terrible way, so I didn't have anything negative to say about them. But I wasn't too happy about this question. I needed something a little more ferocious.

"Your name is Gentle Sparrow," he announced, moving on to the next person.

That was it. There were no more questions. He required no explanation for my answer. Nothing fun. Nothing crazy. I said I liked a fish you could win at a booth in a sketchy fair and the guy named me after a bird.

I didn't say too much about my heritage until the fourth grade. We were learning about local Native American tribes, which in Georgia include the Cherokee tribe and the Creek tribe. Following our unit on Native American history, we were each in charge of making an informational poster about one of the two tribes and presenting it to the class.

Everyone in class seemed pretty fascinated with the Native Americans, so my ego boosted just a smidge and I created a hot pink poster about my people, my clan (the Deer clan), and my name. I tacked a dream catcher onto my bright piece of paper and pasted pictures of me and facts about my Native American naming ceremony all over that thing. I had never been so excited for a teacher to hang up one of my posters. She put it high on the wall, right above my least favorite bully's desk.

I was all giddy, dressed cute to bring in my poster, ready to be cool, until a girl with light brown hair and circle-rimmed glasses, who was sitting right behind me, piped up, "There's no way that's your name!" She cackled and rallied the red-headed bully beside her to join in the joking. Just as quickly as the spark and excitement over my name had kindled, it burned out. I was embarrassed, hoping I could ask the teacher after class to take down my poster, but she didn't take it down for almost three months.

Maybe the girl behind me didn't believe me or my poster because there's a hint of Scottish and Irish in my family, making my skin almost powder white. I mean, that's the only Native American trait I didn't get. Measure my nose. Check out how high my cheekbones are. Snag a strand of my super dark hair. When I put on bronzer, I scream Girl Who Probably Plays with Foxes and Has a Tomahawk in Her Car.

But maybe she didn't believe it because she wasn't at the ceremony. Maybe she was jealous, as most bully tactics reveal. I'll never know why. I was too hurt to ever ask.

What I do know, though, is that people are afraid to be vulnerable because there's a big looming chance they'll be made fun of, looked at weird, or left all alone. Most of the time, it takes only one round in the boxing ring for us to figure this out. We show up with the shiniest of gloves. We have our coach on the side. We're ready to pounce. But once we open up and the other guy hits our weak spot, we're over this whole boxing thing. We call it quits, snatch down the streamers and confetti, and never step foot in the gym again.

For me, my classmates pointing and laughing at my hot pink poster did the trick. I learned to play it safe, only making moves when I was sure it was what everyone else would want me to do. Life seemed less dramatic that way, but deep down, life was much less real. It was empty and lonely because I didn't know who I was, and I chose to be whomever everyone else wanted me to be.

I was only nine when the whole Gentle Sparrow thing blew up in my face, but I carried the fear and shame of being me for years, especially on the dating scene. I didn't bring up the whole Native American thing on a first date, but hiding myself in other ways, with the simplest of things, was an easy, safe tactic. I smiled and nodded my head and agreed. If the boy liked MMA fighting, I loved it. I would shield my boredom with a pretty lipstick grin as I sat with him and his father and pretended to adore the way men beat each other to a pulp. If he thought it was fun to go hunting, I'd hold my pee for five hours, count squirrels, and grin some more. I'd seem just fine sitting at the base of a tree, with no padding and nothing to do but freeze my hind-end off, keep quiet, and play Candy Crush.

As much as I tried to follow their narrative, to play the role they silently assigned to me, all of these guys would still dump me. Even after trying to be everything they wanted me to be, I was all by myself, again. Since I didn't really know or like who I was, I didn't like to be all by myself. Self-discovery takes effort. It takes time to sit with yourself and find out which pieces of you should stay and which should go; that can be hard work. Instead, to keep things easy for myself, I'd add a few white lies to my Facebook bio or cut my hair and try again with the next boy. Healthy, right?

While I didn't appreciate being dumped or abandoned or left on Read, I think the biggest disappointment was that I was terrified to be myself around God. Somehow, I had rationalized a lie that the God Who handmade me and fashioned me into this creature who is worth being nailed to a tree and dying for, didn't know my heart. I didn't know me, so I expected God to not know me. As a 20-year-old girl who had been rejected by classmates and boys, it only made sense that I throw on some fig leaves and mask the most vulnerable pieces of myself around Him too.

Growing up with so much religious betrayal, always trying to toe the line of perfection, it almost seemed safer to not really be me. After all, a real me couldn't mess up. A real me wouldn't have to face God with all of my real shame and real mess-ups. But just like God chased down Adam and Eve amidst the biggest sin to ever ruin the universe, He chases me down. He pursues me with His scarred hands and feet and really soft eyes that see through hurt, and rejection, and loneliness, and sees the wrecked pieces of me I've tried, and sometimes still try so hard, to fit into some other safer mold.

If you've grown up in church, you've probably heard that God's the Potter and we're the clay.

51

*O house of Israel, can I not do with you as this potter has done? declares the LORD.*
*Behold, like the clay in the potter's hand, so are you in my hand, O house of Israel.*
Jeremiah 18:6

Likely, you've heard a message centered around God kneading the wet clay, palming it into shape, and pressing it to its finest on the wheel. But lots of people stop the story with the idea that we have to be smacked and whacked and beat up before we can be the perfect piece of pottery, which alludes to this idea of a perfect ending for the clay. It's as if the piece of pottery reaches a place of perfection on the wheel and is never expected to do anything more besides stay still and look pretty. Honestly, we will never be perfect on this side of heaven, and God hasn't called us to stay put.

God as the Potter never makes mistakes with the perfection He creates on the wheel, but with time, we ourselves chip at the best parts of us. We put the things we don't like about becoming more like Christ on a shelf. We let the pot collect dust, or even worse, we leave ourselves sitting out in the sun as its heat fades our brightest colors.

When dry clay is exposed to the light for long periods of time, the bright orangish-red color fades and the heat eventually causes the clay to burst. God is gracious, patient, and loving enough to let His children fade on their own, if they wish, but He won't let them escape His healing light. He somehow protects and exposes the soul simultaneously, using His light to catalyze a beautiful explosion. His light breaks the pot, shatters the pot, and puts it back together, so it would be a shame to let its beauty fade or to stash it away to collect dust.

"Adam?" That's all He had to ask in the Garden, establishing His authority over creation and sin.

"Mary." That's all He had to say to confirm His resurrection and establish a Kingdom that will have no end.

"Peyton." That's all He has to say because He knows Peyton. Just like Adam's sin, He knows Peyton's sin. He knows all the ways that Peyton has let distractions and judgment keep her on a shelf. Just like Mary looking to belong to Someone real, He gives Peyton a promise that He'll never leave her side. He gives her a reason to get off the wheel and go.

I've never sensed God addressing me with my Native American name. It's never "Gentle Sparrow." It's just "Peyton." But I think God knew what He was doing when old Leather Face asked me if I liked goldfish. While that question didn't seem like it had much to do with the name I was given, God has a way of using some interesting illustrations, much like potters and their clay, to drive His point home.

My dad was named Night Wolf, my mother Yellow Dove, my sister Little Fawn. Wolves, doves, and fawns, and then me, a sparrow. The Bible isn't a fan of wolves; the dove is sent after a twig post-flood, and there's a Psalm about deer panting after water, but have you checked out how many times the Bible focuses on the sparrow?

> Psalm 84:3 says, *Even the sparrow finds a home, and the swallow a nest for herself, where she may lay her young, at your altars, O Lord of hosts, my King and my God.*

> Matthew 10:29 says, *Are not two sparrows sold for a penny? And not one of them will fall to the ground apart from your Father.*

> Luke 12:7 says, *Why, even the hairs of your head are all numbered. Fear not; you are of more value than many sparrows.*

I love how the sparrow always belongs somewhere, even when she feels lonely. What I love most is that her home is at the foot of God's altar, at the place where we are called to be so raw and so real, at the place where we are also called to go and love and serve. That is a place where we fall down, sleep, and wake, in forgiveness, peace, and safety. That is a place where a Gentle Sparrow can be a Gentle Sparrow, where a Peyton can be a Peyton. Where you can be you, without God threatening to leave.

And just think, if the sparrow's home is at the foot of God, and Matthew and Luke say that we are worth way more than the sparrows, isn't it safe to say we are never alone in our constant trial and error, trying to belong, to be known, to blend in, to fade out, so we won't be so alone? If the sparrow is at God's feet, you best bet we are at God's heart. We are in the very center of what prompted Him to send His Son to a wrecked world to die for wrecked people who will never be able to pay Him back.

I'm not saying that I'm always a pro at showing up in the boxing ring for round two and opening myself up to the other guy's low blows, in the fourth-grade classroom, at work, or anywhere else that adulthood takes a whack at me. But when the worst of the worst happens and I get knocked down, I am at the very place, the very altar, the very feet of a God Who wants nothing more than for me to let Him know I got knocked down and I'm willing to go at it again. I'm willing to fight for the identity He's given me, no matter how many people sneer and try to sweep my worth under the rug.

When I'm willing to face my fear of rejection, my inadequacies, my loneliness, God is always meeting me in that space, bringing His altar and placing it at my feet, so I always have a home and I'm always forgiven, no matter where I go or where I fall.

That's a safety net that I'll risk anything for.

# A Spot at the Table

While Josh was gone, my dinners never looked fancy or inviting. There were no lit candles or pretty napkins, only pizza bread and pre-made pasta slapped on a paper plate. I didn't even eat at the table. I always drug a food tray in front of the tv or plopped a bag of popcorn in my lap and called my meal a success. I settled for such a watered down "success" because if I forced myself to set the table, I'd only set it for one. I would reinforce the loneliness if I placed one fork, one spoon, one knife, one glass, one napkin, and one plate on the table. I would have to face the loneliness if I sat at this table and stared at the empty seat across from me. Eating at a table set for one is the epitome of loneliness, and that's something I rarely had the emotional energy to face. But another reason I settled for meager dinners was because I loathe cooking, which comes with valid reasoning that stems from nearly ten years ago:

Blood wouldn't stop seeping through the paper towel, but I kept smiling. My How-To-Cook-Poppyseed-Chicken-Casserole speech couldn't end here. After all, my high-strung, obsessive-compulsive, Enneagram Type 1 existence had a 4.1 GPA to uphold. Unfortunately, after a second paper towel was stained red, the school nurse forced me to throw off my chef's hat and visit the emergency room.

This wasn't the way things were supposed to go; I even hid my thumb and kept yapping about nonsense, as if I were the first person to discover that cream of chicken soup isn't really eaten on its own. My hopes in creating a distraction were a total bust, but on the bright side, the pulsating throb wasn't unbearable yet. Not ten seconds went by before my game of hide-and-seek-the-thumb ended with someone in the back stuttering, "Umm, Peyton? You probably need to stop now and get that looked at..."

My left thumb had gotten in the way of the cream of chicken soup can. When I popped the top and pulled back the lid-- slice! While it didn't feel like I'd done that much damage, two paper towels soaked in blood said otherwise.

An hour later, the emergency room staff glued that bad boy up and I got a tetanus shot.

That day, at 17 years old, I vowed to never cook again. Kitchens would call my name no more. The art of preparing food was suddenly a phobia to me. It ranked up there with marble clowns, Mako sharks, and MRI tunnels.

Needless to say, I kept my word and no longer cooked, until I got married. Then, I tried to fill the sexist role of being the one who always cooked and cleaned until I "volun-told" Josh to start cooking more. But when he moved away, I was left to take that role again.

I hate it now as much as I did when I almost lost my thumb. When life is stressful and racing thoughts pile higher than dusty recipe books, it's easy to let food fall by the wayside. Anxiety, fear, and the need to pace up and down the hallway take precedent; feeding myself only happens when my blood sugar has bottomed and I'm shaking so badly that I can't even make one trip up and down the hallway.

While Josh was gone, what I failed to realize was the simple truth that I didn't have to bring anything to the table besides a willing heart. I could be shaky, hungry, and scared. All God required was a heart that wasn't so self-absorbed, so desperate to get everything right, a heart that was also free to be angry at failure and loneliness. God didn't demand five-star food, flawless thought patterns, or a checklist of the bad things that I hadn't done in order to reserve my spot. There wasn't a holy-rolling bouncer at the dining room door asking where the food was or where I was last Sunday morning. I was an honorary guest just by taking the time to put my heart out in front of Him, and even scarier, in front of myself.

This sounds like an instant release, so easy to accept and live out, but I was handling my loneliness so poorly. I was so trapped by the open invitation I sent to bitterness and exhaustion, that it seemed hard to believe God wasn't upset with the way I was stumbling through isolation. It wasn't that I had put my heart out in front of myself for observation and change, but I wasn't stupid. I knew my heart was in the wrong place. Sure, I also knew God makes room for mistakes, but this mistake was constant, one that I was fully aware of. It was an abusive cycle that I'd thrown myself in, leaving God out of the equation, all for the sake of preserving my pity as ammo and excuses for whatever behavior I wanted to justify.

When people tell me that I'm a good person, my response is always, "But you don't know what goes on in my head." I can be selfish, just like I was when Josh was away for this flight job, but I'm hard on myself at the same time. Because of this knowledge, it's always hard for me to process how easy it is for God to voluntarily stay in my life. When reality wants to blur that line, I take my situation and parallel it to the Bible for my own spiritual sanity.

For those of you who need a constant pick-me-up like I did, check out Luke 7, where Mary Magdalene stumbles through a fancy religious dinner. She falls at the feet of Jesus with nothing other than some expensive fragrances mixed with her cheap prostitution. Not much good that she's showcasing, right? She's stuck in a pretty sad cycle of poor personal choices and desperation. Yet, her small moment of willingness to just be there, to sit with her sin and the Savior Who could save her from her sin, turned into one of the greatest lessons that Christ taught His church during His three-year ministry. To this day, it's still one of the greatest lessons that we are called to walk in.

Plenty of perfect attendance Sunday School goers know the story of Mary Magdalene, Martha, Jesus, and the alabaster box, but it never hurts to recap or even share the story with the newbies:

In Luke 7, Christ is hosting some sort of "Lunch and Learn" with the Pharisees at Simon's house. The Pharisees weren't in love with Christ's message; they just enjoyed hanging around Him in an attempt to trip up His teachings, to find ways that His truths didn't align with what they saw as God's law. Regardless, Martha, Mary's sister, wanted everything to go smoothly. She was running around like a madwoman, cooking food, cleaning tables, trying to make this whole religious luncheon a smashing hit. Where was Mary Magdalene, though? In theory, she should've been helping her sister prepare and serve food. Or with a reputation like hers, she probably shouldn't have shown up at all, even as a waitress. Regardless, she was nowhere to be found.

You don't hear anything out of her for a while, but that's because she's been nestled in the back, scrounging for her one heirloom, an alabaster box full of precious, expensive oil, that she planned to pour on the feet of Jesus. I would imagine that her head was down, that she didn't want to make a scene. But with matted, tangled hair, she found Jesus at the front of a crowded room and spread the ointment all over her Savior, despite the Pharisees, all of the disciples, and everybody else watching.

The scoffers and gaspers didn't matter to Jesus, though. He didn't care that it was actually everyone else causing the scene and glaring at a prostitute sprawled at His feet. He knew from the moment she darted toward Him there would be a beautiful exchange of sin for forgiven shame. Her tears and raw repentance melted the Savior. Just as the alabaster box of ointment was broken for Him, He was broken for her. And in that moment, performance, bitterness, all the selfish stuff she'd done, didn't matter.

Naturally, Martha, the works-over-faith girl, pitched a fit because Mary Magdalene wasn't helping with the cleaning and cooking. Judas Iscariot, being a money miser till his death, had a meltdown because the oil she poured over Jesus' feet could've been bartered to feed hundreds of orphans and widows. Every other Pharisee who had a "calling" to religious, lawful perfection was scanning for the nearest exit because they couldn't be seen in the same one-yard radius as a prostitute. There are so many things "God's people" found wrong with this simple act of showing up, but wait; catch what Jesus says to Simon and all the other nagging naysayers in Mary Magdalene's defense:

> *Then turning toward the woman he [Jesus] said to Simon, "Do you see this woman? I entered your house; you gave me no water for my feet, but she has wet my feet with her tears and wiped them with her hair. You gave me no kiss, but from the time I came in she has not ceased to kiss my feet. You did not anoint my head with oil, but she has anointed my feet with ointment. Therefore, I tell you, her sins, which are many, are forgiven—for she loved much. But he who is forgiven little, loves little."*
> *And he said to her, "Your sins are forgiven."*
> Luke 7:44-48

Mary Magdalene just trumped the most religious crowd in the city. She knocked a stingy disciple into second place all because she was obsessed with Christ. True, she didn't have any big spiritual gifts. She didn't bring any sort of food with her. She spent most of her days selling her body to make ends meet, but she had the courage and enough love for a selfless God to overlook the pointing fingers and gasps, to crawl up next to Him, and to weep. I'm not sure whether she was weeping more over her sins, or more over the fact that Jesus didn't shush her, chide her, or discreetly have her removed. Regardless, lots of intimate things happen when we just stoop down at His feet.

All Jesus wants is for you to show up, tears, heartbreaks, mistakes, loneliness, and all. Why? Because that's when you're most malleable. That's when you bring this to the table: "I can't anymore. I don't want to anymore. I want everything to end." Then, God has this insane ability to say, "Yeah, but I can. What you can't do anymore, put it on me. I want your pain to end too. But I want it to end with your heart full, content, and loved."

When you let Jesus call the shots, the endgame is always beautiful, always giving you the victory.

Sometimes, I think it takes getting to our wits' end to grasp this concept. It takes the ugly moments, the lonely moments, the I'm-crying-on-the-bath-room-floor moments, to wake up this idea. Unbeknownst to me, this truth was hiding deep inside me at an early age. By the time I was 13 years old, my father's Post Traumatic Stress Disorder (PTSD) was in full swing. He'd been diagnosed three times with Traumatic Brain Injury while working as a Georgia State Trooper. He'd had six years of constant brain damage while boxing competitively in the Army, and two or three career-induced car wrecks that emotionally choked his soul. It was hard on me. It was hard on my little sister. It was even harder on my mom to battle alongside him. It's a crushing thing to take on another person's demons, to live in their hell too.

So many days I would come home from school and peek around the living room door to gauge what kind of mood he was in, tired or raging. I would minimize my conversations with him so I wouldn't say anything to trigger his disorder. My father was Jekyll and Hyde, and I was a daughter without her real daddy. There was no more playing Pretty, Pretty Princess with Daddy. There were no more diving board tricks or water ball games. There were no more laughs.

It took nearly seven years of coaxing and encouraging before he sought medical help. After nearly 12 years of Christian counseling, filled with 14 daily hormone pills and countless ugly memories, he's more humble and more God-fearing now than ever. But dang, the soul-cutting memories don't fade.

These were the days when I couldn't bring any "Hey, God, look at what I did today!" conversations to the table. No, I was usually rocking back and forth in my quiet room when I had time to spare. As a young teenager, I had no other prayer than, "God, please don't let my house be chaos. Let Dad be happy." Over the years, though, my prayers have matured. They've turned into the harder prayers, the ones I have to grit my teeth and quickly spout before I can go back and decide not to pray them. Those are the scary prayers like:

"God, I'm so thankful that You always pull through, but how much will I love You when things don't pan out? How will I feel about You when Dad's PTSD never fades? Will I even like You if I can't ever see that fun, glittery brown in Dad's eyes again?"

"God, I know that I vowed to love Josh 'for better or for worse', but the worse is really outweighing the better right now and I'm not sure why You're so okay with me battling a mental disorder with him gone all the time. Where's Your humanity?"

It's the scary answers, tough mantras, that I choose to speak:

"God, I'm so thankful that You always pull through, but I'll still love You when things don't pan out. I won't let my heart harden when Dad's PTSD never fades. I'll love You through the bleak times that don't really fade."

"God, I'm still not okay with being by myself. I'm not okay with the gut-wrenching truth that there's no fix-all button for my OCD. But I'll sit here in the silence and let You spell it all out for me, whenever You're ready. This is Your plan, not mine."

I get this deep pit in my stomach when I mull these questions over and over in my head. I get an even deeper pit in my stomach when I claim to love Him through all things, knowing He's challenged me to live up to these words as a PTSD survivor's daughter and a pilot's wife.

Here's the not-so-scary news, though: This concept, the one you want to bury one-million feet under the ground and forget you prayed about, is the reason it's worth showing up at God's table. When you're willing to wrestle with and hold onto this truth, even when it hurts, then you're actually holding a dinner reservation with promise. It's worth all of the stake-claiming prayers because of this one thing: God never disappoints. Just as hard as I've always tried to impress Him, He's moved my life pieces around to give me hope. While I get exhausted and grow angry from the effort, He is obsessed with the constant opportunity to dump His affection and blessings on me.

Since He's this good, the truth is, I still owe Him the effort of showing up, even when I'm walking up to an empty table set for just me, with boxed pasta and plastic silverware, when it's just a table that doesn't seem to promise much.

This is how I finally figured out why people say, "Keep the faith." It's because, as humans, we don't create faith, we don't sustain faith, we don't bring faith to completion. That's a total Jesus thing. All we can do is clutch faith with the feeble fingers we have. The keeping of faith rests in our ability to accept that He keeps us, not the other way around.

There are so many days when my faith doesn't look like sight restored to the blind. It doesn't look like Peter stomping on stormy waters. Many days, it's my husband and I, blocking each other's phone numbers when we've both said nasty words we can't take back, the kind of words that we should never speak when we're states apart and lonely out of our minds. When that happens, the only thing I can do is sprawl on the floor and sob. It's accepting that following all the rules doesn't mean you'll always have all of the answers. It's spilling water on my laptop, whamming my knee against the doorframe, and touching a hot stove, all within a 30-minute span, and immediately telling God I'm so sorry for all the cuss words that flew through my head and sometimes sneaked out of my mouth.

That's it. That's what my faith looks like 85 percent of the time. But when I look at Christ's faith, when I see Him melt the pride in my marriage, when I hear Him constantly whisper, "You're human. It's okay," I'm overwhelmed with the idea that when all is said and done, my imperfect effort is accepted in His eyes. He's not an all-perfection-or-nothing kind of God. My "e" for "effort" passes His test because He's more attuned to human nature than we realize. When I ask Him where His humanity is, I have to face the truth that

61

His humanity chose to hang on a cross for me. Then, I don't have much room to hurl such a question in His face. Even so, He welcomes my anger and my questions and hands them back restored and answered.

On the days when I've pouted with Josh because he's been gone, the days when I'm too tired to be a good dog mom and take them for a walk, the days when I don't have the energy to make the bed or cook a new meal, as long as I show up with empty hands that are ready to be filled, I'm welcomed with open arms by the Host of Hosts. It's a reassuring thing to know when I'm called to bring something to the table, that "something" is a messed-up, mistake-making me.

It's an honor to know I'm never without dinner company. I never have to eat alone, even when I'm the only human in the room. That's it. Showing up with an attempt at love is the only necessary requirement. The all-access pass to a five-course meal prepared by the One and Only Jesus is mine for the taking.

And it's yours too.

# A Skinny Coyote

While Josh was many states away, Indiana at first, then Florida, I had sole custody of Alfie and Daisy. Not that any court of law mandated this, but without me, those crazy sausage balls were up the creek. They were mine to feed, walk, take to the dog park, love, snuggle, roll my eyes at, and everything in between, including letting them out for potty breaks.

Years ago, humidity bumped Mother Nature off her totem pole in Georgia, so you're either stifling hot or a wet, achy cold, no in between. Georgia winters are rarely brutal by blizzard standards. We don't have snow piling high and shutting us up in our houses, and we shut down school if there's half an inch of snow on the ground or flakes simply floating in the sky. But of course, the one winter that Josh was away, Georgia had one of those bone-aching, miserable seasons.

Each night, when the sun went down, temperatures dropped to the high 20s to low and mid-30s. In theory, this shouldn't be torture, but like I said, Georgia doesn't play. We could feel the wetness in the air as it met the cold, low numbers, suspending ice-like temperatures for everyone to traipse through.

Because I have a mushy heart for animals, I let Alfie and Daisy stay inside while I was at work. I'd make the 20-minute commute home on my lunch break to let them out. This wasn't convenient for many reasons, particularly since it was a daily guessing game of what Alfie and Daisy would destroy while I was gone. This, by the way, included pillows, dog beds, the dog camera, and a priceless, one and only wedding gift from a family member who is no longer with us. Nonetheless, Alfie's thin coat wasn't made to withstand

63

cold temperatures, so I didn't have the heart to kick them out.

However, this minor inconvenience turned into an impossible feat when a coyote showed up in my neighbor's yard. My neighbor at the time was a college professor who taught evening classes at a campus out of town, so he was always either gone or asleep. That meant there was no warning him of the coyote. In fact, it was nearly six months before I even saw him, and that meant he never took an ounce of responsibility for the creature in his backyard. The weight of the matter fell on my already stressed shoulders. Three phone calls to the local marshals didn't do any good, either. Apparently, it's not the marshals' job to help remove coyotes, but you can borrow a cage from them, trap the coyote yourself, and wait for them to pick it up, unless there's a two-week waiting list for a cage. Since there would be no compensation for this feat, outside of a rabid coyote scar if it bit me, I turned down that uncompelling offer. All options exhausted, chunking Alfie and Daisy outside for a quick potty break, while I was on lunch break, turned into a woodland safari that often had me running late getting back to the office.

Every time I let the pups out, I had to walk outside with them, scanning the back of our fence to ensure the coyote wasn't near our property line. Weird thing was, the coyote would go days on end without making a scene. Other days, he'd sprawl in my neighbor's yard, casually basking in the sun for all of Rocky Creek Drive to see. He wasn't a very coyote-like coyote, if that makes sense. Honestly, at first, I thought he was a starved dog. He wasn't with a pack. He didn't have the creepy, thick, hunched back. There was no prowling, snarling, or circling potential prey. The abnormalities had me confused, until I finally caught a glimpse at how skinny he was. Rabid? I'm not sure. I didn't see any foaming at the mouth, but he was the ribcage-showing kind of skinny and didn't mind being seen in the daylight, so something wasn't quite right.

Unfortunately, walking the property and checking for the coyote wasn't just a lunchtime thing. Even when I was at home after work, I would have to stand outside with the dogs, in the freezing weather, especially at night, since this was when coyotes were supposed to be more active. I was the Secret Service in a sweatshirt, with a flashlight for a weapon, while Alfie and Daisy were President and Vice President. They strutted to-and-fro, chasing squirrels, riling up their other dog friends, convincing the neighborhood to vote for them, unafraid and rarely amused by the coyote. Meanwhile, my only mission was to assess the threat, prevent harm, and safely escort them back into the house.

But it was all for nothing. The coyote wasn't that threatening. Like I said, he'd rather sunbathe than attack my dogs. Nice as this was, it still didn't mean he was rabies-free, and I couldn't risk my dogs getting bitten, let alone viciously attacked, especially when I couldn't remember the last time both of my dogs got their rabies shots.

Day after day, night after night, I kept up this annoying routine of clearing the coast and watching every move Alfie, Daisy, and the coyote made, and nothing ever happened.

Most days, the coyote served as a nuisance, but one night, one of those really bitter nights, the coyote struck a softer nerve inside of me. A few weeks earlier, I had noticed that it had made a home in some thin brush in the back of my neighbor's yard. As thin as he was, and as measly as the underbrush was, I knew he had to be freezing. I couldn't fix the freezing part. I wasn't going to get close enough to him to offer a blanket or a doggie sweater. I could at least make sure he wasn't starving, though. Coyote, spider, or any other creepy animal, it still doesn't deserve to be miserable, so I grabbed one of Alfie and Daisy's more expensive treats, a big, thick gnaw bone, and ran it outside to the fence line.

I spotted its glowing eyes near the underbrush, yards away. I'm not very good at throwing, but I hurled that bone toward the coyote. Who knows if the bone reached him? With my sub-par athletic ability, there's a possibility it landed nowhere near him. I told him to stay warm and enjoy the treat anyway.

Much like Rocky the chipmunk, Alfie the punk, and Daisy the sausage ball, the coyote became another critter that melted my heart, even though he took a little while longer to warm me up. He became something I could take care of, something that could distract me while Josh was away. Of course, I wasn't going to let my pups near him, but I couldn't stand the thought of the thin guy going hungry, either. I knew that deep, pit-aching feeling all too well for different reasons, of course, but because of that, I wasn't going to let him suffer anymore than he had to. Sad thing is, I can't recollect seeing him again, as far as my stress-filled, hazy brain can remember. I recall scouting for the bone the next day, trying to see if he'd found it, but I didn't see it. I couldn't find him, either. I grappled with whether it was possible I had given him a bone that choked him or killed him, but I try not to think about that much.

Roswell, Georgia is no place for a country animal or any sort of scavenger like the coyote; they're animals that need plenty of room to roam. There are fancy, two-story restaurants, fixer-upper kinds of houses, and lots of cars everywhere... all the things Peyton and Josh can't really afford. Regardless, it's certainly no place for a coyote. Not that there's really any place for a coyote, but this coyote was different, okay?

One of my biggest fears was that he was run over. This fast-paced, car-zipping city would've made him a frogger, but I never saw any signs of roadkill on the main highway. My next biggest fear was that someone shot him. If he was rabid, this was the best way to put him out of his misery. He looked so skinny and small, though, that he needed to be protected, not killed, at least in my coyote-friendly opinion. My final and biggest fear was that he starved or froze to death. These are the kinds of deaths that take their time. They are slow, but they let you know they're present. It turns into a brutal game in which a player rolls the dice but never gets to move their piece forward, a game that I halfway tried to manipulate and fix with the gnaw bone. It was a game that I never had the power to win.

The worst part of any of these heart-wrenching options was that he was alone. He was all by himself to face some scary things, so in a strange, ironic way, we were in mutual company. Of course, I had a warm, comfy bed to nestle into against the cold winter outside, but deep down, my soul was about as achy and frigid as his little body was. Yes, I had a kitchen full of food: meats, veggies, starches, snacks, the whole lot. But my worn-out body was hurting and hungry, much like his frail belly. I felt as protected as he did in his twig brush. I felt as tired as he did, fighting against his calling to be a ferocious hunter so he could just sprawl out in the grass and do absolutely nothing under a not-so-warm sun.

His was a losing battle. Though I never saw him again, I'm sure he lost his life. While Josh was gone, I lost much of my life too. I had no energy, no drive, no vitality. I found purpose in nothing outside of pure survival. While survival at this point seemed like a prize-worthy goal, I never stopped to think about which pieces of me would die along the way. Were they the pieces of my heart and soul that I needed just as badly as the coyote needed a good meal and a warm place to sleep?

Laughter died. Outside of the occasional joke at the office, I didn't laugh much. I didn't exactly feel lighthearted when I walked into an empty house and knew I would have to clean, cook, care for the dogs, and do everything by myself. There was nothing funny about wondering if someone was going to crawl through the tiny window in the basement and hack me into pieces in the middle of the night, either.

Rest gave up the ghost, not that I've ever taken the time to rest. Survival makes self-care seem weak. Survival seems like it takes grit and guts, but to take a bubble bath while reading a book and sipping coffee, to eat take-out and spend money on a pedicure all in one day seemed like cop-outs. It took away that Joan of Arc feeling I was going for, the feeling I needed to prove my bravery, that merited bitterness.

Empathy faded. Over and over, my brain replayed a personally-scripted narrative: This was hard, I didn't deserve this, and my passive-aggressive expression of hidden emotions wasn't on me. This narrative worked its way into my heart and eventually, I was so frustrated and so consumed with my own problems that I didn't look around at other people who might've needed me. And petty tunnel vision derails you every time. Truth be told, you're only free from the worst parts of yourself when you're investing the best pieces of yourself in others. You can fact check me in Matthew, Mark, Luke, and John's red text.

Laughter, rest, empathy, were all good things that seemed impossible, and their impossibility hinged on my attitude; I was in no mood to twist and turn into anything valuable. I knew, if I made the best of the situation, if I had a good attitude, it would cancel out the validity of my complaints, my fits, and my insults. I knew, if I made this whole thing seem like a near-death experience, survival would be my anthem. Everyone else could let me march in my own self-pity parade. I could use the loneliness to my advantage, no matter how much it hurt anyone else, or me. But selfish schemes never end well, and this little plot would actually turn me into someone that no one liked, including me.

What I didn't realize was, while I thought the pity parties were all to my advantage, I was the coyote, the skinny, lonely mongrel limping toward a slow, painful death. And just like the coyote, I was a nuisance, an inconvenience, and a pitiful heartbreak for everyone else.

***

When Josh was away, my wonderful dad was willing to fight Atlanta traffic, pick me up, and bring me to my parents' house for the weekend. It wasn't a short commute, but the day and a half of being around my family gave me a thread to hang onto. I didn't have to scan the creepy basement or triple check that all the doors were locked before bed. Someone was there to help me watch the dogs. Someone else was cooking. I could semi-sleep in for a few days, but when I was awake, I was no fun to be around.

Mom eventually called me out for being such a complainer. I couldn't enjoy my time with them because I was too busy unloading my misery, unpacking each way this season of life was ruining me, airing out all the ways Josh was failing to be there for me. I made it impossible for them to support and encourage me because, quite frankly, I didn't want encouragement. I wanted them to confirm and validate every ugly feeling I was using to pit myself against any opportunity for growth and change.

Loneliness leaves room for lies and hurt. If you let those things simmer long enough, they spill over into a mess you can't fix. One of the biggest lies I believed was that my mental health, or lack thereof, hinged on Josh's presence. Granted, it's true that loneliness can trigger worse days with my OCD, anxiety, and other symptoms, but I was blaming my adrenal glands' malfunctions on Josh, instead of on a nasty attitude that became my addiction.

Josh was the sole source of my misery, or at least that's the story I chose to tell. It was a story that let me manipulate who the bad guys were, leaving me the unmerited heroine. Truth be told, I was the worst kind of bad guy. I was Scar, who preferred to prowl around Pride Rock, letting my ego and my survivor image reign supreme. All the while, I was hiding the scared, scarred pieces of me I didn't want to reveal.

To reveal your loneliness is to reveal your hurt. It's easy to unpack happiness because it's followed by the good stuff, the things that make your life Facebook-worthy. Not only is it easy to talk about happiness, but we like to showboat our happiness. It fits us into a nice, neat box with a pretty red bow that lets the whole world know what a gift we are. But letting go of anger, frustration, and hurt requires us to recognize that we're wounded, to recognize that we might be snipping and snapping because our heart is breaking. Anger, frustration, and hurt require us to realize that we need a break from the social media standards we place on ourselves. It might make us look human enough to say, "God, I can't survive this one, not without You. And while I'm surviving, can You make sure that I'm a better person on the other side?"

There is nothing more real than a prayer like that. I know this because I tried it, and it worked. Naturally, I didn't harness this game-changer until the very end of my journey through loneliness, but it paved the way for healing. It made me realize that I wasn't just hanging on by a thread. God wasn't just casually throwing me a bone to keep me going. He was giving me the freedom to expose the pieces of me that were begging to heal, the pieces of me that wanted to be content, and even kind. On the flip side of this experience, I can tell you that it's so much easier to speak life to people, to give others the upper hand in the relationship, to let them know their efforts are noticed. It's okay to be vulnerable with everything you're feeling, and it's also okay to have to work at letting go of some parts of you that need to fall by the wayside.

I learned to tell Josh, way after he was home for good, that I understood why he had to be away. I understood that he had to take the only job available, not only so he could pursue his dream, but also so he could provide for us. I learned to admit I was wrong, that deep, deep down, I didn't enjoy being ugly to him. I finally learned that vulnerability meant I could be the weakest and toughest, all at the same time. It's usually a messy look, but it's the only way you get anywhere.

Our first encounter with Jesus is never full of leaps and bounds of glitter and confetti and happiness. Our first encounter with Jesus' salvation requires a messy conversation about how muddled and muddied our lives are. But at the instant we admit this vulnerability, Jesus takes our mess and replaces it with joy and contentment. That trade-off is surefire proof that bitter anger

69

can never live in the same place as pure joy. You have to choose. Jesus requires you to make that decision. You have to be the big girl and choose to let Jesus work through you.

Choose Jesus. Choose contentment. Choose the things that won't starve you out. Even if it's hard, even if it's uncomfortable, even if it wrecks you, just do it. Jesus won't leave you high and dry, hungry and cold, defeated and humiliated. As strange as it might sound, He won't leave the coyote, just as He won't leave the sheep. He's never been One to abandon, cast out, or give up pursuit when it's hard, heart-wrenching, and selfless. That's the space where He meets us, but that's never where He leaves us. He's just that good.

# Dusty Suitcases

As a child, I liked playing hide-and-seek with others, but what I really liked was playing solo games of hide-and-seek. Weird? Maybe, but I loved when I would strategically disappear, holing up in my closet behind my two wooden horses, or standing between the shower curtains to see how long it would take for someone to miss me and come find me. It was a reassurance game for me, a psychological chance to prove that I was loved, not that I ever felt unloved growing up. There was just something about the constant acceptance of someone actively seeking me out that made me feel good about myself.

One of my favorite places to hide at my grandparents' house was behind their bed. They had this thick, cherry wood bed frame with big pillars on all four corners. I was small enough to wedge between the headboard and the wall, so I would crawl back there and hang out where Maw Maw and Pepa kept their suitcases. To my little heart's demise, most people wouldn't come looking for me there. Now I understand that was because my mom and Maw Maw needed an extra cup of coffee and five seconds of silence after putting up with me most days. This was their temporary freedom. So I don't blame them for letting me hide myself away. Truth be told, I usually didn't give them enough time to miss me. I'd get so impatient waiting on someone, anyone, to find me that I would crawl back out of my hiding place and find them, instead.

The impatience came from a place of curiosity, from the realization that while I was staking out, something cooler might be going on, and I couldn't miss out on something cooler! As it turns out, I was usually just missing out on a few lukewarm cups of coffee while Mom and Maw Maw enjoyed the post-Peyton quiet. Still, I think we always like to know what's going on because it gives us room to occupy the same space as others. Either Mom found me or I found her (the more likely option); regardless, we were in the same place.

When we're in the same place as someone else, we tend to feel more normal. Most of the time, we see normality as the good cancelling out the bad. It's a calm quiet that we've created, a label that somehow validates the routines and explanations for all the things we do. If everyone else spends five hours a day on Instagram, then it's totally normal that I'm spending five hours a day on Instagram. It's not an unhealthy, mindless way to compare my life to everyone else's; it's just normal, right? If everyone else thinks it's acceptable to randomly stop texting someone, then it's not emotionally abusive or long-term damaging for me to just not text him back or answer his calls, right? That's just what you do when you don't like someone, right? If everyone else accepts that pity parties of loneliness are justified, then I'm not being a jerk. I'm just being normal, right?

We don't realize it, but "normal" becomes a weird justification process that invites us into a stagnant cycle of bleh.

***

Josh planned a little North Georgia road trip for the two of us not too long ago, just to get our travel fix amidst a pandemic. It was an outdoorsy, minimalist agenda that would make the CDC proud, so I stepped a smidge outside my comfort zone and grabbed several masks. Josh purchased extra hand-sanitizer and some peanut butter cups, and we were off.

One of my and Josh's favorite things to sightsee is old, dilapidated churches. We love the ivy-laden buildings with white, chipped steeples. I'm a firm believer that there's Holy Spirit power that still surges through the old bones of churches built on good, strong foundations.

There were plenty of old churches scattered through the countryside as we wound our way in and out of narrow roads and around mountainside views. Most of the churches were still active and had signs showing all their worship times and the pastor's name. Church sign sayings, the short quote-like blurbs, make me feel all sorts of ways. Some are too fire-and-brimstone to really minister to anyone, some are misspelled, and others have it together.

One of the signs said, "God gets ordinary people for extraordinary jobs." While my knowledge of basic Christian phrases agreed with that, another side of me felt unsure, uneasy.

The truth is, God doesn't call ordinary people, because ordinary people don't exist. While I am a firm believer that God makes all of us unique and special, I'm talking about the grittier details that set us apart, the flip side of fun, special, and glittery things that make up who we are. I'm talking about the fears, traumas, and failures that have shaped us, the things that make us unique in a darker way.

We live in a strange culture that encourages us to embrace why we're different. Yet, this same culture creates social media platforms that force us into identically filtered bubbles that demand we all live life so we breach at least 100 likes on every social media post. "Be you, but be cool enough." That's what the 2020 monster of culture and conformity whispers every time I log onto any of my social media accounts. "Show just enough of your failures to look real, but mask enough of that stuff to be liked. What you can't use to your favor, pack up in an old dusty suitcase and shove it behind your bed. No one will see the problems there, not even you." That's the overall message.

I've made enough mistakes, thought enough nasty, atrocious things, thanks to sin and my OCD, that I know I'll never be cool enough. Won't happen. Not because I couldn't fake it, but because my most basic understanding of "cool" is that something has simmered down, the heat was released. And that doesn't sit well with me.

When I was born, Mom says the nurses taped a sign to my little hospital bed that said "Wild Thing." Five minutes into this world, I made it clear I didn't like a pacifier and my feet were my favorite weapon. I kicked and hollered, kicked and spit out my pacifier, kicked and hollered, kicked and hit a nurse in the face with my pacifier. I was more than a wild thing; I was a wildfire with nothing calm, cool, or chill about me.

This world needs wild, passionate people to get the job done. Often, these people are wildfires, thanks to the nightmares they've been through. If you don't believe me, you might want to check out John the Baptist. This dude ate bugs and honey, wore some interesting clothes, was a social outcast without a home, and yet, this was the man Jesus picked to pave the way for His ministry. You have to be a wildfire. You have to sweep in and say the consuming things, the intense things, especially when they're part of who you are. You have to wear your identity, no matter how rugged, hairy, or charred it may seem. You can't avoid the mental health crisis you try to hide. You can't forget about the divorce your parents went through, or the breakup that has you questioning why you weren't enough. You have to care enough about others that your own hurt, your own sort of not-so-normal, becomes a way for someone to find God's healing too.

For the longest time, before I understood the real meaning of OCD, I just thought I was a worrier. That's the label I had given myself, the label everyone else had given me. For a while, being a worrier felt normal. It was a social disclaimer most of society had come to accept, even parallel with progress, success, and carefulness. Lots of people volunteer themselves for this category, but deep down, all along, I knew my worrying was too different, too intense. It didn't fit everyone else's standard definition. For 13 years, I stuck a generic worrier's label on my life and shook off the intensity to everyone, but deep down, I felt so alone. This was the kind of worrying, the kind of crazy, raging thoughts, that would make someone cuff you with zip ties and throw you in a shrink's office. So I kept it all to myself.

No one needed to know about my Harm OCD, that I was always afraid I had run someone off the road. I would turn my car around to the very spot where I had the thought, just to ensure no pedestrians were laid out in the street and no cars were nose down in the ditch. No one needed to know about my Sexual OCD. No one needed to know I was so afraid I would, one day, somehow cheat on Josh, so I would awkwardly sit on my hands in public and clench my teeth so I wouldn't say or do anything scandalous. No one needed to know how scared I was to change a baby's diaper, because all my thoughts were always inspired by the ridiculous, but somehow convincing lie: I was forever bad and would forever want to do bad things. A murderer, adulteress, child abuser, germaphobe-- I bore all of these labels that were not so pretty, not so good, not something I ever wanted anyone else to know anything about.

While Josh and I were dating, I was able to suppress the OCD tendencies. Dating bliss and positive distractions usually quiet the "crazy." Once we got married and responsibilities grew, OCD's most refined ammunition came out of nowhere, essentially detonating my life. Paying a new mortgage added financial stress, staying up late to cook and clean for two added physical stress, avoiding arguments and playing the eternal, blushing bride added emotional stress. A new label added new requirements and I couldn't keep up with them. It was too much, not that Josh put that pressure on me. Society and self were to blame.

As a new wife, I kept an arm's distance from the idea of therapy. I'd never liked the idea of sitting in a room, on an obnoxiously comfortable couch, surrounded by framed diplomas with some sane person's name and insanely sane accomplishments emblazoned on them, only to spill to them that I'm nowhere near sane. Therapy was for weak people, right? The strong ones survive without weekly chit chats about their struggles. Besides, if I decided to go to therapy a few months into being a new wife, either Josh would think he'd married a crazy, or that he'd somehow sent me off the deep end. I continued to keep quiet, holing myself up in the bathroom at one in the morning, four in the morning, whenever I was alone, so I could have whatever meltdown I needed, without Josh or the rest of the world knowing.

But God didn't want to leave me on the bathroom floor, so He sent me Wendi.

Josh has always known how much I like words, books, and reading. He's always known how much I wanted to be an author too. It's been a dream of mine for a while, so being the goal-driven kind of guy that he is, he did some networking for me while he was at his first job as a sales rep for the Atlanta Falcons' football team. Turns out, his boss' wife was an author, and once the boys started talking and realized both of their wives loved Jesus, liked iced coffee, and really had a thing for words, they thought we should meet.

Wendi invited me to Taproom Coffee, the most industrial, hip coffee shop in all of Atlanta. It was lovely. I ordered an earthy matcha green tea to add to my own hipster, green flare. I decided, one sip in, that matcha was the worst mistake of my life, but I wasn't going to let Wendi know that. She was nice enough to pay for the nasty thing. Good news was, we talked so much that I didn't really have to drink anymore of that gritty green mess. We talked about

Jesus, about Wendi's daughter, Lucy, and about our husbands' jobs with the Falcons. We talked about words, her books, my writing dreams, and then we talked about harder stuff.

I wish I could remember the exact words Wendi said, but she didn't mind looking me in the face and saying, "I have Intrusive Thought OCD." She started telling me about the random, wild thoughts her brain had, how hard they could be to push through, and just how strong and present God was through it all.

And then *boom*! That was it, those were the same thoughts my brain was thinking, the ones in which I'm always afraid I'd run someone off the road while I was driving. Those were the same thoughts in which I'd be so afraid of harming a baby that changing their diaper sent my brain into overdrive. The same ones that were so intense that I was not sure why God had stayed.

The same ones that were the same as someone else's. The same ones that made me feel not normal but made me feel healed through the abnormality. I wasn't alone anymore, only because someone else let God use their grittier, more raw, not-so-normal story for something extraordinary.

In a way, I think God sent me my own John the Baptist. Granted, Wendi wore super cute clothes and didn't eat bugs or drink honey, but she didn't mind speaking the wild, hot truth. She didn't mind looking different and ignoring culture's boxes of normality. God told her to share her story to pave the way for my healing. Because of God and Wendi's willingness, I found freedom. I saw a bigger, better picture of a God Who loves.

This didn't make my OCD go away. Trust me, I have to practice putting my OCD in timeout every second of every day, but God has given me this new sense of grace. He's given me His grace to see my OCD, my mental health battle that so many people falsely label, as the chance to prove how good He is at staying. He's given me the freedom to step outside of social media's demands and society's rules. Now I see there are some differences that, though they feel like hell, are actually a glimpse of Him, of heaven.

Several months ago, I had the honor of speaking on Wendi's podcast, *Soooo OCD*. One of the things I told her was, if dealing with OCD helped me feel God, then it was worth it. If it took the awkward explanations about why my good girl rep was down the drain, thanks to a mental breakdown, it was worth it. I said it was worth it because He was worth it.

So sure, I have no doubt that God can call ordinary people to fulfill some extraordinary things. After all, He's God and can do whatever He wants. But I think He prefers to use the outcast pieces of us to play a bigger part in His story. There's no need to pack up and push away the trauma, the failures, and the hurt. Don't let those parts of you collect dust, much like the suitcases behind my grandparents' cherry wood bed. Odds are, when you use your story to make others feel less alone, you'll recognize that God is healing you too.

Invite someone to get coffee. Ask them to join you for a walk. Start the conversation right where your gut doesn't want to, and watch God round it off with a peace you couldn't foster on your own.

Go on. I dare you.

# Spinning Airplanes

I've never been one to drink, not even when loneliness drove me to almost anything that would numb my mind. On my 21st birthday, I went out for pasta and soda. When I was in college, I crashed sorority events and was the girl they told to just hold an empty solo cup so all the guys would leave me alone. (FYI: The frat guys won't ever leave you alone, solo cup or not. I had one follow me to *my* car so he could drive me home...) The wild side never hit me, so I couldn't land the role of Leading Boozer at anyone's party; neither had I mastered the art of tolerating more than an ounce of alcohol.

That's not to say that I'd never had alcohol. As a southern child raised in the sticks, alcohol was a homemade pharmacy for the sick:

"I'm not drinking that stuff. It's wrong to--." I choked. But down it went, a tablespoon of fire water curing my aching throat, clogged nose, and burning forehead.

At ten years old, I remember my Maw Maw's hand on her hip and the discreet smile creeping up on her lips as she demanded that I chug her mother's remedy of home-brewed moonshine, mixed with honey and peppermint, to cure my pre-flu infection. My great-grandfather may or may not have run an illegal moonshine distillery on his property back in the day, so the homemade remedies were always a smidge intense, and still are. Not that they ever fixed the problem, they just knocked me out long enough that I slept off whatever germs I had.

Maw Maw always got a kick out of watching my pupils dilate and my ears spout smoke while the alcohol shocked my body, but, boy, if she could've seen what that wild concoction would do to me 13 years later...

78

The morning after your wedding is when you're supposed to wake up in an array of love and rose petals. I woke up with a sweaty fever, chills, and aches all over. Only four hours of airtime stood between me and what was supposed to be the best winter wonderland vacation of my life, yet there was nothing romantic in sight for my stuffy nose and raw throat.

After I drudged through airport security, flung my ticket at the check-in lady, and found my uncomfortable seat, I plopped down and prayed that this cold, this flu, this Ebola, *whatever*, would just vanish. Shortly after, my prayer was answered when a flight attendant wheeled a cart full of potent beverages down the aisle.

Josh had surprised me and upgraded our flight from cheap, cramped status to Delta® Comfort. Fancy, right? Right. The seats weren't soft, but I got unlimited access to the snack bar and any sort of drink that I wanted. As the flight attendant pushed a cart of initially-not-so tempting alcohol down the aisle, I recalled my family's homemade antidote for chills, aches, and fevers, the same recipe that my Maw Maw used on me. Hard liquor would be an instant fix, but one I hadn't tried in a while.

With too much encouragement from my husband, I whispered to the flight attendant, "Excuse me, ma'am."

Her dull, I'll-pretend-to-love-my-job smile thinned. "May I help you?"

"I want two mini shot bottles of Jack Daniels."

I felt so drained, so icky, so tired of being afraid of missing out on my honeymoon.

Without thinking of any sort of aftermath, I tipped the first bottle back and chugged the whole thing.

I don't chug alcohol.

I don't sip alcohol.

I. Don't. Drink. Alcohol.

Especially not on an empty stomach.

But that didn't stop me from prepping the second bottle for some Coke Zero® to finish off my own pharmaceutical fix. Less than 30 seconds later, I couldn't stop laughing at anything, laughing at everything, and then, laughing at nothing. Anger swept over me once I couldn't sit up, once I couldn't see, once the happy drunk me turned into the mad drunk me. It didn't take five minutes for me to turn into one of the immature frat guys I had hated in college, the person who was an adult and volunteered to consume a drink that would create the most obnoxious, petty person ever.

After Josh shoved some flavorless granola bars and even more flavorless almonds down my throat, I picked up my legs, yes, literally picked them up with my hands, and hobbled to the tiny airplane bathroom, grappling for seats, whacking people in the head to steady my travel. Using an airplane bathroom while drunk is kind of like being thrown in a spaceship without gravity or any astronaut training, having forgotten to attach your galactic catheter. No fun, especially when you've always been terrified of the unsanitary conditions of an airplane bathroom. Apparently, while no other cognitive functions work when you're drunk, OCD still does. Go figure.

Stumbling back to my seat, I mumbled a new prayer that the Lord would just let the Ebola bacteria take me. I don't remember this part, but according to Josh, I looked at him with a furrowed brow and viciously yelled, "This is your fault!" I can't imagine making a scene, but he says it was loud enough for everyone to hear. At least I was entertaining, right?

A few minutes after I pointed that shaky finger and blamed Josh, the airplane dipped and ducked, swinging back and forth to prep for landing. This was miserable stuff when the world was already spinning. I fought nausea for what felt like ages until Josh tucked his arms under me and dragged me off the plane.

I found a table outside an airport café and called my mother to confess my sin and cry. About an hour later, the hormones, exhaustion, toxicity, or maybe a combination of all three, dissolved, and I realized I could breathe out of my nose. My throat no longer hurt and everything was focused again. I wasn't unjustifiably angry at anyone, either. Once I proved to myself that I could exit the airport without assistance, I let loose and laughed along with Josh, realizing that Maw Maw's old-school remedy had done the trick once again.

God extended some extra grace that day and taught me a sobering lesson on moderation.

At first, that's as much as I took away from that experience. For the longest time, it has served as not much more than entertainment when Josh and I feel like being funny, but there's more to the lessons learned.

Fact is, we like quick fixes more than we like healing, and there's a big difference. Quick fixes are when Josh gets attacked by a German Shepherd and thinks the puncture wounds half an inch into his finger only need some peroxide and a band aid. A quick fix is when Peyton thinks liquor will cure the flu and solve a honeymoon crisis, even though, less than a day later, I had a terrible nosebleed and all sorts of other problems. Quick fixes leave the wound wide open for hours, sometimes for days on end, giving infection plenty of time to make its move. Quick fixes leave jagged scars that never fully stop hurting. Sure, they stifle and hide the ugly, oozing parts, but there's usually a soul price to pay.

God made the body in a cool way. He's given us these nerves and cells that always know what to do when crises arise. Did you know the second your skin is scratched open, cells flock to the wound to start building new layers of skin? It's a God-engineered miracle machine that doesn't need you or anybody else to kick-start its works. The process is fascinating, mind-blowing, and instant, but the results aren't. And that's where we get stuck. We prefer the end goal as fast as possible because it doesn't require us to work on it ourselves. I mean, it would be great if we could wake up one morning and casually run a marathon, but we can't do that. Our bodies operate on systems, and most of those systems require training and time.

Our souls require time to heal too. Scary, hurtful life moments can happen out of nowhere, and in seconds, life can unravel, but we aren't put back together so easily. As cliché as it may sound, God doesn't want us put back together again overnight, because He's doing something with the pieces. I don't know if this is how God works, but I think before He puts the pieces back together, He shifts them around. He arranges them to fit in a tighter, stronger space than before. I think there are some pieces He sweeps up and chunks out of our lives too. Honestly, I think there are a few pieces He busts up into even more pieces so they can be shifted and rearranged and put into their perfect, God-sized place.

This was particularly hard for me to face as a constantly confused, young adult, but I eventually learned that God isn't afraid of breaking my heart if healing is the end result. As much as I have wanted to fight that, I've seen it work.

When all of the yucky, flu-like symptoms dissolved, I thought my honeymoon was going to be surefire fun the whole time. But, no, it didn't happen that way. I'm pretty sure Josh and I fought at least once a day while we were

81

on our honeymoon. I was battling my undiagnosed OCD, which I've now learned is always triggered by drastic life changes, like marriage. Fast fixes don't fix you or your life. And if fast fixes don't fix you or your life, you're still broken and busted up, pretending everything is fine, when even the slightest gust of wind will shatter you to pieces. And if God needs you to come to grips with a mental disorder, if it's time for you to humble up inside a therapist's office, He'll keep busting up your heart until you cave.

I thought I would be fine when Josh moved away for his flight job. I knew how to defend myself, cook for myself, and occupy my time. But once I was all alone and could see how bitter I was within my loneliness, I had only two options: I could keep sitting with my bitterness and hating everything or face my own mess and start letting God heal me. I had to sit with myself in the quiet, stare myself down in the mirror, and force myself to have a better attitude. This didn't happen overnight. Lots of times, I'd have a great outlook on Josh being gone, as far as his getting more flight hours and getting to an airline quicker, but as soon as he called me five minutes later than he was supposed to, I was just angry. Angry at him. Angry at my loneliness, and most important, angry at my own anger which wasn't coming from the right place.

Now, I was never angry with God. I was too smart for that game, but I wasn't too thrilled that He didn't just fix my bitterness and loneliness. "Why?" I would ask Him over and over again. "Why am I by myself?" Some days, I could just accept that He was doing this for a reason and move on. Other days, I felt like a worm on a hook, bobbing in the ocean, letting it toss and turn and flip me until I drowned or something ate me alive.

In the middle of it all, I never got a specific answer from Him. When you ask me why I was alone, I can tell you what I learned, but I can't give you a surefire why. It was more of an "I'm working on you," which didn't always propel me to behave like a big girl. I didn't want to be worked on. If I had to be worked on, that meant something wasn't working right, and I was always right, at least that's what I thought. After all, I was always the good girl who got all the good grades and always kept her virginity and character in line.

What I failed to realize, that I see now in hindsight, was that I was hearing from God, and that should have been enough of an answer. He didn't always want to have the same negative conversations that I wanted to have, but He was letting me know that life didn't spin out of control without His permission. Contrary to cheesy devotions and watered-down teachings, God will let your life tailspin out of your control. Let me reiterate: Life will not spin out of His control, but out of *your* control. He'll let you stumble and bumble and wallow into the messiest places possible, so simply hearing His voice becomes your salvation, becomes the very thing you'll fight for until your last breath. Just knowing you have a lifeline to the God of everything is more than you deserve, and sometimes, He'll let you walk through the fire to see that.

Does that answer always sound fun? No. Do I still remind God I'm in no mood for a Job kind of life? Yes. But if God craves a relationship with you more than He craves your constant goodness, then you're safe to fight through the highs and lows of surrender.

I kept asking God, "Why?" and He kept saying, "It's for a good reason." Eventually, this became what I looked forward to. I didn't look for answers as hard as I started looking within myself, seeing where I could be a better human, seeing if maybe, just maybe, it wasn't about Josh leaving. Rather, it was about God shifting my heart's pieces and putting them back where they were supposed to be. Now, let me remind you, this took a long time to figure out. To this day, I have not mastered this. I still have to fight to make this practice a consistent, daily part of reality.

Bitterness is a parasite I've hosted for a long time. It's easy to work with bitterness because it boosts the ego. It reminds you that things aren't your fault so it's not your job to fix them. But when you're all by yourself, and things start falling apart, you can't really turn around and blame your husband who isn't there. You can't blame the neighbor you don't know. You can't blame your girlfriends who are miles away. You can't blame a God Who is kind enough to buckle up and hold on while you spin out of control. You have to gently take responsibility for hurt and bitterness, not because life hasn't dealt you a bad hand or people haven't given you a reason to be broken, but because God wants to put you back together.

You have to be willing to squirm and wrestle with yourself for a while; you have to be willing to ask God some hard questions and expect some vague answers. But in due time, you'll realize the answer is always God filling every crack and cranny of your heart that's been left wounded and open for so long.

83

And if He's always fixing you, then it's never on you to find a millisecond cure-all for life. Pressure's off you; it's put on a God Who knows that when the pressure is on, He'll take the beating, the bruising, and the morbidity of life. It is through His power alone that He'll provide the healing.

# Green Tea & Therapy

Silence is strength, or at least that was the false truth most of my family members forced themselves to accept. It was a lead-by-example sort of tactic I inherited. I come from a good ol' southern family of farmers who learned to keep their acres by training hunting dogs and running an illegal distillery. They could milk a cow, skin a deer, shoot a squirrel, attend Sunday morning service, and take a swig of fire water, all in one fell swoop. Oliver, my great-grandfather, always posted a tobacco spit can beside his chair at the head of the dinner table, while Bonelle, my great-grandmother, churned butter and stitched water can patterns on thin cotton dresses. The fridge was always stocked with a gallon of sweet tea and leftover homemade blackberry pie. Meanwhile, my favorite candied orange slices were hiding in a heavy glass jar behind the dining room door. I'd pick a slew of wild daisies growing out by the storm pit, leap past the front porch rocking chairs, and snag at least three or four of those candies at a clip.

Bonnie Sue, my Maw Maw, who despises her middle name, is the oldest of Oliver and Bonelle's six children, three boys and three girls. All three boys were drafted into the Vietnam War, all gone at the same time. All three returned home with stories they have forever refused to tell. Occasionally, a memory will slip, but only because one brother is sharing the trauma of another. They don't ever tell their own stories. One of them has a purple heart, his legs overtaken with shrapnel that doctors couldn't remove. Makes him sound tough, invincible, but it would shatter your heart to watch him walk through his backyard to feed his chickens, his shoulders hunched, his gait slow and measured.

Another brother was ordered to hop out of his unit's truck and run a simple errand. Just a few steps later, the truck rolled over a mine and all of his men were blown to smithereens. All alone for days on end, he stumbled through the thick, steamy jungles of Vietnam. The elements got the best of him and he collapsed under the weight of exhaustion and dehydration. He later woke to a Vietnamese refugee woman who fed him dog soup until he regained his strength enough to travel on and find more US troops. For decades, he has drowned this memory with bottle after bottle, addicted to the numbness. Last time I saw him, he was so intoxicated that he told me the same thing about seven times.

And the other brother, well, I haven't heard any of his stories yet. I'm not sure that I want to hear more of the stories anyway.

I've heard these true tales from my mom, who heard them from my grandmother, who heard them from whichever brother the story wasn't about. Silence for these men was strength; it was a way to dodge the trauma without admitting they might have to trudge through it, much like the bamboo and fog of their very hellhole. Boxing up the past meant there would be no breakdowns, no tears, and no one to see the mess, but there would always be nightmares, faces paired with memories, and the emotional damage that can't hide with all the mothballed uniforms and rusted badges that stay hidden in the closet. To talk about it would be to unearth the reality of death, war, starvation, mangled humans, all the stuff our senses want to shut off, but I think our brains know we can't sensor experiences. We must let them be what they were. At the same time, we can heal from them, grow from them, and share them for the sake of another.

But as life goes, one generation tends to teach the next generation both the good and the bad. My great-grandfather taught his boys to be "men," the kind of men who don't talk about problems. In turn, they taught their boys to be tough. And in turn, the third generation, my generation of boys and girls, has been taught to pull ourselves up by our bootstraps and just deal with life. This sounds like quite the mantra. It looks sharp, brave, and daring, but the reality is, we can't pull ourselves up by our own bootstraps when life doesn't hand us a boot or it snags our shoestrings before we can cinch things up.

My family thought it best to teach me to glare life in the face, to scare it so it wouldn't scare me, but there are times when we aren't called to be mean and amped up. There are times when we won't have the energy, the emotional capacity, to fight. And no one ever told me this, but it's okay to not be the tough kid.

It's okay to hurt. It's okay to cry. It's okay to fall off your bike and cry and cry and cry until the sting goes away. It's okay to tell your dad with PTSD that you're not okay when he's not himself. You can say, "Hey, you're not you, and my little heart is breaking into pieces, but it's not my job to pick them up and put them back together." You can say that you saw men die, women get slaughtered, and children manipulated into carrying guns and marching into battle. You can break down, because at the end of the day, your breakdown turns into the very thing God uses to pick you back up.

Weakness produces humility, whether we work with it or not. Eventually, when we tap into our weaknesses, we see God's goodness. We find a little fuel, light the fire He's built, and let Him jolt us back on our feet. And the best part of that? We know we'll get knocked back down, but it'll all be okay. In short, it's okay to not be okay. The weight of the world has already been carried.

I didn't know these things before, though. All I knew was that I had grown up in a strict church that taught me God was more concerned with the rules than with my heart. I was either wearing a long skirt or I was showcasing my knees and making Him angry. I was either reading the King James Bible or reading some "evil" translation that was a little easier to understand. God was either using a megaphone to call me to follow more rules, or I was too sinful to hear His soft, good voice. Those are some tough lessons for a child to learn, especially when they were never meant to be taught those lessons. But I thought God wanted me to pull myself up by my bootstraps and deal with life too. I thought, if I didn't pull things together nice and tight, wrap my life in a pretty bow, then He wasn't pleased. This false perception of God wired my brain to be afraid of Him, to be afraid of the very One Whose love casts out fear.

I didn't talk about it. If I mentioned my fear, I must be in the wrong. No one else around me at the church seemed bothered by God's apparent lack of sympathy, so maybe He was as gray and looming as they painted Him to be.

87

And maybe I was supposed to love Him for it, but that felt impossible.

I didn't know that it was okay to feel dismay when Josh left for almost four months. All I knew was that I had grown up in a culture that taught me that women were meant to sit in the quiet, pin all the right bobby pins, bake all the homemade things, and just grin while the men took on the world. But there was no one to cook for, no reason to look presentable anymore, and I was left wondering why everyone stifled my feeling of being utterly lost, why no one said, "Yep, this suck. And you are safe to feel unsafe."

So, I talked about it, but not much. Every time I mentioned how frustrating the whole thing was, I was told I should think long-term, see how Josh was trying to provide. No one else around me seemed agonized over my loneliness, so maybe I was the green, nasty witch who was always mad.

***

It shouldn't shock you that going to therapy had always seemed like a failure to me, like I couldn't handle life on my own. I was that girl who had to see a "shrink" or visit the "psych ward." That meant I couldn't destroy the darkness on my own, that I was puny, ignorant, and defeated. But loneliness, OCD, and trauma had created a tornado and I was caught in it, spinning nowhere, leaving more destruction in my path. Regardless of the way I grew up, the way people stereotyped therapy, I sought help because I finally realized that silence was not strength. It only muted the mess; I might not have heard the noise, but life was still playing. Bad stuff was still happening, and I was not strong for ignoring what was there. Silence was an isolating, self-shaming demise. And if I didn't talk, if I didn't unearth where I was coming from, I would eventually regret waking up and look forward to going to sleep. And that's a scary, empty place to be. Trust me, I know.

I swallowed my pride, shucked what I was taught, and made the appointment. I put on a good front when I first introduced myself to my therapist. I wore professional clothes, smiled when I was supposed to, and accepted a cup of hot green tea when she offered it. I held that hot cup in my hands, trembling from all the stress. I held onto it and didn't want to put it down. It felt good to touch something normal while I was in such a different place, a space that felt too peaceful and soothing for my out-of-control emotions.

Karen, my therapist, started the session simply by asking about me, which was a heavy-laden question when I had to unpack trauma, OCD tendencies, and a stubborn assumption that I was a failure for showing up. But I started telling her about growing up with a father with PTSD, dating a boy who was emotionally abusive, and attending a church that taught me God would never love me until I did x, y, and z. Turns out, that was all considered trauma, and trauma serves as OCD's perfect petri dish. That's where it thrives, grows, and morphs into a bigger monster.

Being away from Josh, being all by myself, meant that my brain actually did a healthy thing: It pulled all of my boxed up hurt, and the shame of feeling hurt, out from under my bed. It dusted off the lies, and it slung the top open. It spilled out all the ugly truth onto the floor, leaving me the job of figuring out which things needed to go, which needed to stay, and which needed lots of work. But all those things were too much to process separately. Traumas have a way of intertwining and ganging up on you, and I was too tired to process alone.

I've always liked the idea of work, of doing things to prove I was worthwhile, to prove I could hunt down my own boots, lace them up nice and tight, and dig deep into the grain of life. The thing about therapy work, though, is that it requires you to sit with what you're feeling. That doesn't mean your actions are always justified, but it means you can say something hurts when it hurts. You can say something is unjust when it's unjust. You can say you were wronged when you were wronged. And you can sit with God in the anger and sadness, the fire and ice, of all those feelings.

I'm not sure why I wore makeup to therapy as long as I did. Maybe it was because I believed the lie that it was something of a joke, maybe I was still trying to hide the dark circles under my eyes and the stress acne cratering my face. But time and time again, I left that place with less mascara than I had on when I walked in. Eventually, on the first day, I put down the cup of lukewarm tea that I never drank because I found a release in talking about the ways life had done me wrong. I found a release in someone saying that churches can be wrong, loneliness can fuel anger, and what I was feeling was healthy. Trust me, I hadn't felt healthy, mentally, emotionally, or physically, since Josh left.

Not that therapy was God, but God definitely started using these sessions as an avenue of grace I'd never given myself. Those sessions became a safe space where I could heal without the mandate that I scuff up my boots to showcase some falsified strength or tie my shoestrings even tighter to prove how my life was full of order. I didn't have to yank and tug and fight hurt. I could just sit with what I was feeling. Instead of therapy solving any physical problems, God used those moments to heal me, emotionally and spiritually.

What is the best insight from God about the healing? It doesn't happen all at once. It's not a constant uphill gradient. It's not a pair of boots with straps and strings and extra rubber padding. It's not a one-time fix-all; there will be ups and downs. What God wanted me to understand about this sort of healing was that it never ended, that healing usually burst scabs and reopened wounds. There will be more hurt, more mistakes, and more pain along the way, but we're safe if the healing process isn't in our hands. We're safe to mess up, to stay silent when we should speak, to sit down when we should stand up. As long as we talk and put our mistakes and hurt and pain in front of us, God can start bagging up the trash and polishing the stuff that stays.

Silence is not strength. Strength is not avoiding therapy. Therapy is not the healing. The healing is God, a very personal God Who knows we need the room to say we aren't okay, a very personal God Who doesn't get impatient when we can't get a grip on trauma or life problems. After all, Jesus came to earth because He knew things were not okay. He knew we were not okay and He wanted a relationship with us. He desires the kind of real relationship that means we can have the broken, angry, frustrated, scary conversations that don't seem to have a resolution. He came to be that resolution, to show us it's okay to point out the injustice, to recognize the hurt, and to speak when everyone else is too scared to call out the heart problems.

He came to sit in our mess with us and let us know there's an eternal place with Him where there won't be a mess. But until then, He's okay when we sit in a chair, cry our eyes out, and say, "I'm not okay." That fuels His fire, the kind of fire that doesn't scorch us or leave a pile of ashes. This is the kind of heat that purifies and heals us.

Let the words out. Let them hurt. And never forget that God feels your hurt, understands your hurt, sent His Son to embody your hurt on a tree, and He promises that you are not alone in the agony.

# Cuss Words & Prayers

I was never good at being good while I was alone, because I never realized that goodness wasn't my whole identity.

In middle school, I was the goodie two-shoes, the "Miss Holier Than Thou," or at least that's what one boy in my class called me. Standing in an empty middle school hallway, surrounded by obnoxious, bright yellow walls, his words shattered my heart. I'm sure he bullied me because so many other kids bullied him, but I was too young to understand that people who hurt, hurt people, and that he was lashing out with lies instead of speaking with kindness. It hurt so badly because I wasn't trying to be high and mighty; I just figured if Jesus was willing to die for us, we might owe it to Him to follow the rules. After all, I was taught that's what a good Christian does. She only follows the rules, neglecting the connection between head and heart.

In high school, I was the obsessive nerd. I worried about my grades. It was Honors Literature or AP History, or it didn't count. There was a lot of crying and there were a lot of late nights, but somehow that helped me land the title of Valedictorian of Lafayette Christian School's Class of 2012. Except, like I've said before, who cares now? Honestly, it's an unsettling feeling to have a decent achievement like that, knowing other big moves I'm making, even slaving over, now might later look just as bleak and bleh as being valedictorian.

In college, I was "Hanners with the V-card." I'll never forget the night my entire sorority found out that I'd made it to 19 without having sex. We were at a sisterhood retreat, camping in the middle of nowhere, and by nowhere,

I mean a sorority sister's parents' backyard. We were playing an Alpha Omicron Pi version of Never Have I Ever. As soon as someone mentioned sex, my little tail didn't move, because never had I ever had sex. As soon as one of the girls realized that I hadn't gotten up and scrambled for another seat, she blasted that reality to the top of the pine trees. And from there on out, I was seen as innocent, sweet, and pure.

This sounds great, but when everyone sees you as a parallel to the Lamb of God, it's dangerous, because you're not the Lamb of God. Let's lay this out plain and simple: Peyton Garland is most definitely not the Lamb of God. I'll never match up to the beauty and perfection of a God Who daily chooses to save the weakest, meanest, nastiest pieces of us all. But when people unknowingly give you that god-like reputation, you feel a pressure to be a person you will never be.

For a while, it was easy to be a goodie two-shoes because life was easy. Life was good. Sure, my father's PTSD presented a gray patch in my life, and yes, my first love never loved me back. There were tough times, but life itself wasn't heavy-laden with hopelessness. I got nearly everything I asked for-- all the toys, the volleyball camps, and the brand-new red car. The blessings didn't stop in high school. I got a full ride to college. In fact, I was paid to go to college. I got the Big that I wanted in my sorority. And the one wild-haired tattoo idea I had never made it past the sharpie design on my ankle. Like I said, life was easy; life was good, until I graduated college. Then the realities of adulthood settled in. Stuff got hard; stuff got hard *fast*.

I realized the bare necessities of adulthood, like the fact you might think you're going to make $1,000 a paycheck, but taxes eat up almost half of that, leaving you with maybe $650. And just when you stick with a job long enough to reap the benefits of a decent paycheck, you get kicked off your parents' insurance and lose another chunk of change. I realized some harsher realities too. My virginity and strong Christian faith weren't a turn-on anymore. Instead, they were what kept guys at arm's distance from me. I didn't have sorority sisters and classmates to constantly put me on a pedestal, so the hype of being a good girl was no longer attainable, leaving me empty and lonely.

Eventually, I met Josh, a one-in-one-million kind of dude, who got a kick out of the challenge of waiting to have sex until marriage. We strategically went on lots of hikes and adventures that would make us too tired to even want to have sex. We managed this for about half of a year. Got engaged. Got married in another half of a year. And *bam*! We made it!

Most girls, including myself at the time, think that marrying a man will make life's pieces fall into place. It seems you'll have an unending train of love notes scattered on the kitchen counter or taped to the bathroom mirror. Or you'll always have someone there to listen every time you cry and need to vent. But here's the truth: You'll pick up more pairs of his dirty socks strewn all over the floor than all the love notes you'll ever receive. Odds are, when you start to cry, he'll panic and find an excuse to duck and dodge a discussion about emotions. I'm not saying all men are like this all the time, nor am I hating on Josh. What I'm saying is, while we make plans for Prince Charming, we marry an imperfect man, a creature we have to remind not only to talk about his feelings, but also to bathe.

Aside from the distracting humor, there I was: I had reached every classy, Southern woman's "dream" to be married and fulfill her wifely duties, but it left me a little less than fully satisfied. Life still wasn't perfect. I still wasn't perfect. There were still bills to pay, late nights with tv dinners, and advanced degree classes on hold. I was learning to overwork myself, frustrate myself, and throw a wooden stirring spoon when I was tired of cooking. Sure, I had Josh to face reality with me, but that's just it-- I still had to face reality.

The pedestal wasn't enough anymore. Being a bride wasn't enough anymore, either. I got all I ever wanted, but I was still aching for something fuller. Since life wasn't making the cut, I got really tired of bringing my best, hoping some-one liked it enough to validate me. Even when I did the work and people labeled it "good," everything was still empty. And I was left by myself to figure out why I was so hollow. Long story short, pride convinced me to be selfish, and selfishness had drilled a deep hole through all the good parts of me. The worst part was, I was clueless.

Part of reality, part of a real, healthy marriage, is putting your spouse above your own wants. After all, that's what love is. Now, that doesn't mean you hang out in an abusive relationship or tolerate disrespect, but it does mean you vowed to God to be this man's teammate, the kind of teammate who's willing to pass the ball and let the other player make the winning shot. So, when Josh came home and said, out of the blue one day, "I think I want to be a pilot," I said what I thought every good wife should say. I said, "Okay."

As I mentioned before, Josh had a wonderful, steady job as a sales rep for the Atlanta Falcons football team. It was a nine-to-five sort of gig that came with some pretty commission checks.

It provided us with a healthy rhythm of financial gains and a schedule we could count on. This was a job worth bragging about, a job that included bougie trips to Atlanta. But only a few months in, it left Josh feeling unsatisfied. He knew this wouldn't reap any eternal benefits, but as a pilot, there might be more opportunities to help people, to carry missionaries overseas, or deliver doctors to their hospitals.

This made worlds of sense to me, so I was all on board. The timeline was simple: Josh completes school in nine months, earns leftover flight hours for roughly a year, makes it to Delta. I could manage that. That was pretty short-term, until it wasn't.

Weather is a big deal when you're a new pilot. If you barely know how to start the engine, it's not the best thing in the world for you to fly through heavy wind and rain. When Josh started flight school in October, he fell into a rainy winter season. That pushed his flight hours behind for almost three months. In the grand scheme of things, three months isn't that long, but when you're the only one bringing home a paycheck while he's in school, three months of waiting gets a little stressful. My body doesn't handle stress well. I get tense quickly, and my tension is a live wire, just waiting for the tiniest thing to set it off.

Taking a second job to balance out the bills was the spark that caused total combustion on the inside, but my angry, external fit didn't happen all at once. Rather, the smoke seeped out in tiny, petty ways. When we didn't have the money to buy two dozen oatmeal raisin cookies from my favorite bakery, I made sure Josh knew it was because of him. When we didn't have the money for me to pay for a book or get my nails done, I blamed Josh. When we couldn't make any big, long-term plans to pay off his student debt, I let him know it was his fault. I made snide comments, offered snarky suggestions, and pushed my independent agenda on him.

I was no longer Miss Holier Than Thou. I was a punk, and the scariest part of that was, I had never been good at holiness. Instead, I'd just been good at cruising through a life without hurdles. Now, with hurdles in my way, I was

94

face-planting on the track, scraping my knees, and bloodying my nose every step of the way.

Josh was gracious through it all, bandaging up my knees, pressing ice to my nose rather than showing me my big, pouting flaws that were already consuming me. What I quickly learned was, while Josh was a student, while he was home much more than normal, I felt so alone. My fears had turned into frustrations; those frustrations turned into anger, and anger was choking the life out of me. It was yanking me away from the truth, where healing was. It was blinding me to the way God was using Josh to help patch me up each day. I had let isolation overshadow healing.

I carried that anger the entire time Josh was a flight student. Once he finished flight school, I thought I would lay that bitterness down, but the second his new flight instructing job left me alone, physically alone, I slung that bag of bitterness up and over my back with a vengeance. If I could prove just how heavy this burden was, I would come out the strong one, the brave one, the good one, the one who hung around. Meanwhile, Josh gallivanted toward a pilot dream that had yet to prove any benefit for me. Since I could no longer worship my goodness, I could worship my survival skills, or so I thought.

Here's the truth: If you survive while others fall at your feet hurt, mangled, and used, who wins? Nobody. Who deserves the title as a strong, brave, independent survivor? It certainly was not I.

Left alone in a quiet house with a creepy basement, while Josh was away for his new job, made me not like myself. I was in this grueling cycle of justifying my anger with more anger, justifying insults with the proof I was reaping nothing from this experience. Over and over, night after night, I would try and fail to ignore the truth whispering in my ear, "You know, you really aren't handling this right. It'd be much easier for you to just let this go."

Letting go is freeing, but I think we get really comfortable with our grip, even if we're gripping something we know is toxic. Toxic things are toxic. No duh, right? But if we stick close to something that's toxic, we can blame all the bad on what's toxic, because everyone knows toxicity is bad. We can point fingers at everything but ourselves.

You can't do that when you're stuck by yourself all the time.

When you're angry with yourself, you tend to let it out on others. That's no secret, but I think we dismiss the idea that we might just hurl some angry prayers to God in these seasons too. Not that I was ever angry at God for Josh leaving. I've learned there's never a point to getting angry at God, but the prayers I hurled at that time became tense. They became so tense that Miss Holier Than Thou started dumping cuss words into her prayers.

I'm not much of a cusser. I didn't grow up around it. Cuss words never felt right rolling off my tongue. Still, as weird as this sounds, it felt different when I prayed. Let me explain: I had so many meltdowns in that house that I can't remember what launched such an angry prayer. I do remember finding myself in the hallway, an empty space where I'd yet to hang any happy pictures. I started wringing my hands, clenching them into fists, throwing them around as anger pulsed through my body.

"WHAT," I stomped my foot. "IN" stomp. "THE" stomp. "HELL" stomp. "ARE" stomp. "YOU" stomp. "DOING" stomp. "HERE?" I hurled at God.

I threw up my hands to Him, popping an attitude the same way I did back in 2007, when my dad looked at my faded jean capris and told me they were too tight and I had to change clothes.

I was rude to God, more than rude. I was literally posting up on Him, as if I somehow could back Him into a corner. While that was by no means right, while it's never okay to sling around ugly words, I realized something. I just opened the door to my heart to be more raw and real with God than I had been in a while, maybe in my whole life. We weren't separated by rules and a realm between heaven and earth. He had become so real to me that I found Him to be a safe space to let out every bit of my anger and hurt. Sounds scary to say, but the amount of peace I felt after praying that way was indescribable.

Funny thing is, He never really told me what in the h*** He was doing. Instead, as it is with His good kind of love, He showed me that He stays, that He gets me, and that there's no better place to be a Not So Miss Holier Than Thou than at His feet. There's no better place to be a washed-up valedictorian than at His feet. There's no better place to be the virgin who's no longer a virgin because she's now a sucky, bitter, married woman than at His feet.

Just a few days ago, I heard one of my favorite pastors, Brad Thompson, quote a Bible verse I'd never noticed in Job. So often, when we "know" the Bible stories, we neglect the chance to open ourselves up to learn.

Job 13:15 says, *Though He slay me, I will hope in Him; yet I will argue my ways to His face.*

I wasn't sure how to take that verse at first, because I knew that God doesn't slay His people. In fact, He slays anyone who messes with His children. But I think what God was getting at was that He slays the pieces of us that have to go. I'm over here cussing in a prayer as He's slaying away my anger and hurt. I'm stomping around on the ground, acting like a total brat, while He's slaying the aching loneliness. And maybe I have the context all sorts of wrong, but God allowed what Job said "… yet I will argue my ways to His face," to appear in the Bible. Job knew that God was working on him, but Job still wanted God to know he was not cool with that. And the best part is, I'm pretty sure God was cool with Job not being cool with everything going on. He let Job's humanity spill out into the Bible so you and I would know He's a God Who not only fixes our humanity, but also sits with who we are in the process.

He won't leave us unhealed, but in the moments when we are too scared and tired to work with Him, He'll grab His first-aid kit and start pouring antiseptic on the wound, letting us yell and argue as He cleans us and protects us from any further damage. Eventually, He'll add some salve and a band aid, and one day we'll see a jank scar that means something eternal. It will be a scar we look for in the bathroom mirror as a reminder that God is Jehovah-Rapha, the God Who Heals.

So, in truth, I guess I can tell you what He was doing. He was healing my heart, healing my loneliness, healing my worst shots at love and goodness with Himself, the very source of love and goodness.

# The God with the War Ax

I grew up in a family that absolutely loves Jesus. Because of that, I know Jesus today. My Maw Maw was a Sunday School teacher; my Pepa was the head of the Board of Deacons; my Mom was an Awana leader; my Dad was a church security team leader, and my little sister was the girl who got the most bizarre prayers answered at a rapid-fire pace, every single time. If she lost any of her toys, she would ask God to help her find them and they would turn up in my bedroom not five minutes later. If not for these people and their raw love for God, the church where I grew up would have scared me away from Him all together.

While I've already highlighted some of the lows of growing up in this church, there are even more gritty details you have to understand:

If anyone mentions a revival, homecoming celebration, or anything old school, my palms sweat, my right leg bounces uncontrollably, and I have to leave the premises immediately. If I have a dream about the church where I grew up, I cannot go to church or pick up my Bible that day. I wake up in an eerie, damning fog that won't let me focus on God.

I grew up going to a brick and mortar, countryside church where heavy rules were stacked sky high. This church taught me a few harsh lessons about God that never lined up with the Bible, but since I was usually afraid to read the Bible, I took the church leaders for their word. Their peculiar list of rules was as follows:

1.  Women are not allowed to wear pants to church. Long hair, long skirts, and minimal makeup preferred. This "don't wear pants" rule

later equated to "whoring around," which sparked some not-so-gracious sermons from behind the pulpit.

2.  If you use any other Bible translation outside of the KJV, you are going to hell. Seriously, it was that harsh. If you brought in an NIV or ESV Bible, you were headed to the stake. Not sure if they thought Jesus was doing the condemning, or if they got some sort of sick kick out of threatening people with this sort of stuff. (More than likely, they never did their research and realized the pompous inspiration behind the King James translation.)

3.  Women cannot lead worship, and contemporary Christian music is about nothing but folks getting a chance to flaunt themselves and dance around onstage. After all, this contemporary music is nothing but the same few words repeated over and over. But as I remember, the young man leading worship all the time was hitting up all the females in the church after the service. So was it only women who are so sexualized and immoral? And aren't most of the Psalms and the angels' choruses a series of phrases repeated over and over?

    Revelation 4:8 says, *Day and night they never stop saying: 'Holy, holy, holy is the Lord God Almighty, who was, and is, and is to come. You are worthy, our Lord and God, to receive glory and honor and power, for you created all things, and by your will they were created and have their being.*

4.  If God doesn't smite you over the head and write your name on a wall, if your salvation story isn't that dramatic, God hasn't saved you. In fact, if you want to know Jesus, you can't just approach Him and ask for a relationship with Him. You must wait for the writing on the wall before you have the true right to come to Jesus. As if any of us humans will ever have earned the right to come to God, apart from Jesus' simple request:

    *Come to me all who labor and are heavy laden, and I will give you rest. Take my yoke upon you, and learn from me, for I am gentle and lowly in heart, and you will find rest for your souls.* Matthew 11:28-29

As a child, before this church catalyzed my Taboo Thoughts and Mental Rituals, I had always had other little OCD ticks, like an obsession with symmetry. If I took two steps with my right leg, I had to take two steps with my left leg. If I took five steps between two sidewalk cracks, I had to take five steps between the next two sidewalk cracks. If I didn't do this, I'd have to return and complete the steps correctly. And if I got any grade below a 95, anything I deemed an ounce less than perfection, I couldn't let go of it. This wasn't just a straight A's sort of thing; this was an unhealthy obsession that killed my physical and mental health. Such a failure ruined my after-school trips to the gas station to get a cola icee. Every time. Constantly washing my hands, counting my steps, calculating my GPAs, and waiting for hell to swallow me up were a lot for a child to carry. By a lot, I mean too much.

By the age of 13, this terrorizing list of church rules had twisted my brain that already ran too fast, already demanded all my ducks be lined up in a perfect row, with perfectly groomed feathers that were a perfect shade of yellow. And even when all the ducks did all those things just right, I was taught that God still needed to hurl down a thunderbolt of approval to symbolize that all of my ducks were quacking all the right quacks.

Scared of not seeing any big signs of approval, I began playing it safe; I packed up my ducks and stayed home. If there were no ducks in the pond, nothing could go wrong. But when my brain ran super, super fast and fixated on ways I could send myself to hell, sitting in my room, alone with a bunch of nonexistent ducks, didn't seem like the healthiest choice.

So, I spent most of my high school career terrified to not be alone, and also terrified to be alone. When I was alone, my condemning thoughts got too loud, but when I was around other people, my heart raced too fast with comparisons. I wondered why that person seemed so at peace with God when I knew I was better at God's rules than they were. I could never stop any of the crazy whirlwinds in my head, so naturally, I had to become a drug-dealing gang-banger.

Just kidding. But I quickly found myself dependent on benadryl, almost like an addict. Okay, yes, I was a benadryl addict. I would pop two of those little pink pills every night because that was the only way I could tolerate being by myself long enough to fall asleep. Without the medicine, it wasn't out of the ordinary for me to be wide awake at 4 a.m., terrified that I had done all the wrong things and hadn't prayed enough of the right things. Since I couldn't see God feeding the 5,000 at my school lunch table, or telling the storm of condemnation in my bathtub to shut up, I assumed He wasn't with me at all. It wasn't even the ache of loneliness, but the pure silence of being by myself in my bedroom, even with loved ones just across the hallway, and I quickly became aligned with shakes, fear, and all things bad.

I don't like to give the devil any credit. He neither has that power, nor does he deserve any of my headspace. Still, I think he knows, if we can be scared of being alone and sitting in the quiet, we won't take the time to listen to God. Instead, we can turn to scrolling through the same Instagram feed we've been scrolling through all day, comparing our lives to other people's lives, wondering why our contouring skills don't match hers, or asking how he has all of this money to travel all the time. We fall into this mind-numbing cycle of self-hate and self-shame. Instead of sitting with God in the quiet, so He can heal our hearts and heads, we keep our minds busy with this same lifeless process. And yet, we question why there are so many memes and GIFS about how tired everyone is all of the time.

I speak this because I've lived it. I speak this because I still fight it. Every day.

If I have to sit in the quiet, I have to think through some deep stuff. When I've already watched *Mulan* twice in a row, and my iPhone is dead, the scary, awkward, crazy things that I've buried somewhere deep in the back of my brain have time to emerge. Legit, I picture these things like zombies popping up and out of the dirt. They are half-dead things because I've ignored them for so long, but they're half-alive because I've never laid them to rest.

And here's the thing: The only way to kill a zombie is to poke a big hole in its brain. The same works for the hard stuff we never wrestled through. Until we face the loneliness and poke a big hole in the fear and the hurt, the aches and weight of life don't go away.

It didn't take long, but because of some heavy religious betrayal growing up, I found out there were too many zombies and not enough ammo in my own tiny, tattered satchel. Meanwhile, sitting alone in my living room for four months, too tired and empty to fight for myself, I learned that the Holy Spirit has some seriously good aim, and He's always packing. You won't always feel this promise. You won't always see it. When you're traumatized, your senses tend to dull, but here's a few spiritual sure shots you can bank on:

101

*Kapow!* Down goes the lie that I can't feel safe in any Baptist church, especially the ones with red carpet, big, fake flowers everywhere, and the stained-glass windows that make Jesus look as white as my legs in mid-December.

*Kapow!* Down goes the fear that sleeping alone tonight will swallow me up!

*Kapow!* Down goes the hurt that says being by myself means I have to attend a self-hate party, the kind I thought God always hosted, even though He had never disapproved of my ducks, my efforts, and all my perfect goals.

If this sounds a little too cliché for you, if you doubt God's ability to outpower your zombies, check out Psalms 35:1-4:

> *Oppose those who oppose me, Lord, and fight those who fight against me! Take your shield and armor and come to my rescue. Lift up your spear and war ax against those who pursue me. Promise that you will save me. May those who try to kill me be defeated and disgraced! May those who plot against me be turned back and confused!*

I mean, God doesn't just have an old, rusted ax that He uses to cut firewood. God has a WAR AX. WAR AXES KILL ZOMBIES. LIKE, DROVES OF ZOMBIES GO DOWN ALL AT ONCE, PEOPLE!

And what I love so much about verse three is that David asks God to keep him safe because David knows what it's like to be alone. This isn't his first lone ranger rodeo. David knows that in his desolation, when every human surrounding him wants him dead, the God with the war ax is on his side. He has sat in fear, in grief, in the face of death, and the God with the war ax has never missed a shot. David knows the zombies will be destroyed and laid to rest.

Yet, David wouldn't know these great truths if he had no other option than to be alone with the worst parts of himself. I wouldn't know these great truths if I didn't have to curl up on my bed alone, or buckle in the middle of the hallway, to face the worst parts of everything the lies, confusion, and impatient people behind me at the red light hurled my way.

Cool enough, David wraps up Psalm 35 in verse 28 by returning the favor. Just as David had asked the God with the war ax to keep a promise, David turns around and gives his own promise to the God with the war ax:

> *Then I will proclaim your righteousness, and I will praise you all day long.*

David realized that the God with the war ax wasn't outside just fighting off the zombies, but He was also shielding David from the lie that he was too messy to be protected. This doesn't mean David actually felt worthy, because when we're in the middle of life's bleh, it's hard to feel worthy. But rather than focusing on where he was and how he would continue to drop the ball, David lifted His eyes to the God Who was dropping zombies left and right.

So, get behind the God with the war ax, the God Who is really good at head-shot kills. He doesn't require you to haul His ammo around. He doesn't even make you run through the crossfire. Instead, He asks you to stay behind Him and sing a song if you want. He asks you to sit in the still and quiet and loneliness long enough to see Him destroy your biggest enemies, even if those biggest enemies are your self-shame, self-harm, or self-hate. He wins the battle. He wins your soul. And while He might be dirtied from the fight, He pretties up your heart and protects it for eternity.

He's good like that, isn't He?

# Baby Steps

After my father became a reservist with the US Navy, he pursued a full-time career as a Georgia State Trooper. While he was away training for nine months, Mom and I lived with my grandparents. Since I was the queen of their world, I was four-year-old royalty every day, for the most part. I walked around in a sparkly crown and "clippy-cloppy" high-heels. Maw Maw let me steal her lipstick and clip-on earrings. Pepa let me put flower clips in his hair and throw glitter wherever I wanted. But even in the middle of this piece of a fairytale, my crown felt heavy. My clippy-cloppy shoes were hard to walk in. The clip-on earrings gave me a headache.

Even this young, my mind was already a live wire, so my little body felt the weight and hurt of the simplest things. In kindergarten, while most kids got in trouble for not turning their work in at all, I would get in trouble for turning my work in with holes all over the pages. I would trace my letters over and over, erasing each time my pencil couldn't follow the lines just right. Over and over, I would erase and rewrite my letters until I had rubbed holes through the paper. Most students would get red marks because they skipped a letter or traced their letters as if their pencils were race cars zooming around the Atlanta Motor Speedway. I got red marks for trying to do everything just right.

In addition to my dress-up games and kindergarten failures, I kept a running list of all the things I did wrong. I would get my little mental list ready at the kitchen table, and before I could walk down the hallway, I thought a mean thought and had to ditch the list. Maybe I told someone to "shut up" in my head, or maybe I thought I hated God, because that's a pretty typical thought for someone with Religious OCD. Then, all of a sudden, the list was pointless. It had to go. After all, who wants a "Wrong Things List" that's slammed full? I wanted to show the clean slate to Mom and Maw Maw at the end of every day. I wanted them to be proud. But that was always blemished five minutes into my quest for perfection. A list of all the wrong things I had done was only proof I had failed to make my day perfect.

Eventually, I stopped making lists. They were exhausting and defeating. Instead, I ran to the bathroom as soon as I thought a bad thought, or did something I deemed sinful, so I could ask for immediate forgiveness. That way, technically, I always had a clean slate. Sounds childish, silly, impossible, but OCD captivates its victims at a young age. It puts every detail of every day on a balancing scale of justice. Right or wrong around every corner. Decisions must be made. And if the wrong decision is made, instant forgiveness is demanded. This routine began when I was around seven or eight, and it only got worse as time marched on.

In high school, I was known as "Pee" (not "P," which would actually make sense for someone named Peyton), because I was always holed up alone in the bathroom. I have the old notebooks and Facebook messages to prove the nickname status. Between every class, at least twice a day during class, and about five times before every volleyball game, I was in the bathroom. So, while "Pee" might not be the coolest high school nickname a girl could get by with, it was the safest name for me. I took the title and ran with it, white-lying my way through four years with, "Oh, I just have a small bladder." But I didn't have a small bladder; I had a fragile, frightened heart that was always trying to cover my dirty tracks with mounds of pure white snow. I remember missing pep-rallies, New Year's Eve midnight celebrations, all the fun things, because I had ducked out in a bathroom, convincing God I was just trying to be perfect for Him.

I didn't understand progress. I couldn't process how baby steps were okay, and failures were expected along the way. I had no clue that God didn't have His own list of "Peyton's Rights and Wrongs." He didn't, and doesn't, operate that way. But a four-year-old girl's desire to be princess-perfect, mixed with heavy bouts of OCD, mixed with a church's lies that I had to walk God's tightrope, led me to believe God was nothing more than a referee. God wore a thick black-and-white striped shirt. There was no room for gray or anything else in between. He blew a whistle and yelled at people to stay inside the lines. He threw up big red flags and told people they were no longer allowed to play the game, but I tried my hardest to play the game right. I wanted to win so I could prove I had a trophy to place at His feet.

I've since learned that God does not like games, just like Mom always told me. Rolling dice, moving pawns, tallying everyone's points isn't what He's about. At the end of the day, without His Son, none of us win anyway. It's that simple. And because Jesus made forgiveness so simple, God isn't scared of the gray. He isn't ashamed of my baby steps that don't always guarantee success. He's not throwing red flags my way, or holding His breath just hoping my spinner lands on the right number. In God's world, there's no such thing as "Do not pass go. Do not collect $200." We all get a free pass because our freedom has already been bought.

Obviously, this is where Paul steps in and says in Romans 6:1-2:

> *What shall we say then? Are we to continue in sin that grace may abound? By no means! How can we who died to sin still live in it?*

This reminds us that we don't necessarily have the greenlight to turn into head-banging party junkies. Meanwhile, He has created a journey for His children, making a start to finish product that requires wrong turns and mess-ups in between. We are required to grow and learn. As humans, we don't do that too well without messing up or coming up against something that over-powers us.

I know I messed up a lot while Josh was gone. Bitterness rooted fast. I started blaming him for my hurt and loneliness. "If I was standing next to an air-plane, there's no doubt you'd pick it over me!" I would yell at him on the phone. "Don't be surprised if when you get back, I'm not here," I would threaten him. I was hurting so much that the easiest fix was to make him hurt more than I was. If I knew he was hurting just as much as I was, I felt I had the upper hand in owning why I had the right to pitch fits, throw hairbrushes, stomp up and down halls, and threaten to pack my bags. If he could feel as badly as I felt, if someone else could validate the level of my pain, then my tantrums were justified and leaving was acceptable, or so I thought. But since when has running from something true and real ever left us anything but exhausted and lost?

Exhausted and lost. That's how I felt while he was away. I was so hurt, messing up so many times, still trying to process that God wasn't angry at my emotions. Rather, He was just waiting for me to see His hand at work, His hand teaching me to hold my tongue, to react in compassion, to see the people around me as friends and not punching bags. And until all those deep things clicked, He hung out with me on the couch, where I was usually crying and cocooned in a blanket. He laid beside me while I was all alone in my bed, tossing and turning and trying to ignore every little noise that my brain convinced my ears it had heard. He was there through it all. While "through it all" usually sounds like cataclysmic events and whirlwind experiences, "through it all" was through all the nothingness. But in my world the nothingness was everything. The nothingness was my emptiness, my hurt, and through it all, He sat with me, unafraid of my fear.

While the baby steps He guided me through were so simple, that's what He used to sustain me until Josh was home. Most days, it took every ounce of energy in my body to convince me I needed to walk from my bed into the kitchen and at least heat up some leftover pasta that I made four days before. Feeding myself was a small victory. It's one He was championing for me. Most days, Mom tried to explain that I couldn't dump this situation on Josh, that it was something out of his control. So, every time I had the guts to swallow my pride and apologize for my rude breakdowns, it was a small victory. It's one He was cheering on. Most days, I didn't want to leave the house. It was less work for my brain if I just stayed curled up in a small corner of my quiet house, but with each little ride with the dogs to get a Puppacinno, with each stroll down the same store aisles, I won a small victory. It's one He was singing over me.

Perhaps why Jesus was so overjoyed to be near children while He was on earth was because they were so honest and owned their mistakes in such big ways. Children own small victories in such big ways too. If they can't handle the bike without training wheels, they will smash full-force into the pavement and tell the story of their nasty scab for the next two months at the dinner table. If they learn to handle the bike without training wheels, they will line all their stuffed animals along the edge of the cul-de-sac to witness the miracle. There will be finish lines and confetti and cupcakes to celebrate the wins, but big stories and big conversations for the losses.

107

I think Jesus wants us to treat each day with the same honesty that kids treat each day. I don't think He wants me to keep a list of my rights and wrongs out of fear, thinking He'll crumble up my meager successes and much bigger failures and throw them all away. I think He just wants me to say, "Hey, I gave today my best shot, but anger got the better of me. I'm sorry. I know I botched things up. Are you up for trying again with me tomorrow?" On the flip side, when we do the simplest of things right, I don't think it sets an even higher bar, forcing us to always one-up our own best moves. Rather, I think He lines up all His angels at the edge of heaven and gently forces them to clap for me. Instead of more rules and bigger expectations, He wants me to come to Him and say, "Hey, I decided to step outside, get in my car, and go for a drive. I'm rewarding myself with some hot tea. You wanna ride with me and chat?"

I have so much freedom to mess up in this Christian life that it terrifies me.

*Terrifies* me.

At 26, I still round off tons of prayers with, "I've given You every reason to run. Promise me You're staying, that You aren't going anywhere." A piece of me will always want to hold my breath, waiting for Him to pack up and tell me He's outta here. But He keeps staying. He hasn't left. He's not as hostile and threatening as I am with Josh. And I'm finding that each time I want to end a prayer with the slightest notion that He won't stick around, He usually wraps the prayer up before I do with a "Have I left you yet?"

So, I think this is where the word "faith" comes into play. You know, the word we all want monogrammed on our purses and tattooed on our wrists, but never want to put into practice? For the longest time, I felt I solely had to bank on what God said, like I couldn't stick around to see if He walked His talk. But, when I finally wasn't as afraid to read the Bible for myself, after months and months of being all by myself, I discovered that I can bank on not only Who God says He is, but on Who He truly is. I've witnessed what it means for Him to never leave or forsake me. He's proven Himself over and over, so I have Someone I can count on, besides myself and all my tainted lists of rights and wrongs.

Let me be clear: This doesn't mean I don't have meltdowns over not being perfect. Just call Josh or Kelly. They have plenty of stories about how I cry when I feel like I can't scrub my toilets enough to make them truly disinfected, or when I think I've accidentally poisoned the dogs because I sprayed kitchen cleaner too close to their bowls. I don't think OCD will ever let me be truly free of meltdowns. Even for you without OCD, the truth is, life won't ever let you be free of chaos and crazy times that make us all feel unhinged, alone, and confused.

Until we wade through those waters or trudge through those deserts, until we show up and mess up, and show up and take baby steps again, we can only hang onto the Bible's words. Of course, the Bible's words are enough, but those words didn't run deeply in my veins until God hung with me through the bad weather and proved everything He's ever said. And that's real love, the kind that is tried and tested and true.

***

I didn't have an official boyfriend until I was a sophomore in college, but before I get into any stories about him, for the sake of his privacy, let's call him Lug. Lug was a handsome Marine covered in tattoos who had just returned home from a deployment in Afghanistan. Thanks to my wonderful father, I always had a soft spot for military men covered in tattoos. Lug's stepmom decided to play matchmaker and strategically brought him to church so we could casually meet.

A few weeks later, Lug and I went on our first date and I was instantly all about puppy love. Lug hung the moon. Lug was the pot of gold at the end of the rainbow. Lug was the male version of a unicorn, all things sparkly and magical. Until he wasn't. Verbal and emotional abuse are real, and when a handsome man sneaks "I love you" in between so much lying and cheating and undermining, it's really hard to bank on anyone else who repeats those words. If love stung so badly for so long, why should I trust it again?

I felt that way for years, and sometimes, that fear still creeps up in my marriage. Josh, my mom, even my therapist, have helped me realize that trusting people is not my best trait. I want people to prove their loyalty and love, and I want them to prove it over and over again. Sometimes, I'll pitch fits, push buttons, and test boundaries to make sure Josh means that he's staying. I know when his patience is thin. I know what words will hurt most. When I am mentally and emotionally weak, I'll use those immature tools to confirm that even when I'm the one to shove him to the edge of a cliff, he'll jump off if it's the only way to prove that he still loves me.

I used this vantage point the most while he was away, when I was drained from always being by myself. And while I have no doubt he loved me then and loves me now, his love couldn't hold up the way God's did. Josh would get angry and we would get in arguments. He would avoid conversation and any discussions around home, because we couldn't communicate properly.

But God let me say whatever I wanted, threaten Him whenever I wanted, cry, cuss, throw things, stomp, spit, everything bad, and when my little tornado fits were through, He was sitting there loving me, and He always knew what to say. It was not usually something bizarre or prophetic. It was the basic things that people tend to say to one another and rarely follow through on.

God said a lot of, "Hang in there. I'm working on you. I'm doing this for you." He promised me, "I love you. Just cry. It's okay." He let me feel whatever I was feeling in that moment, even when it was wrong, and He just stayed. He showed me all the beautiful things that encompass love, like loyalty, honesty, patience, and kindness, over and over.

I pushed so many boundaries, tainted so many lists of wrongs, that if He were ever going to leave, it would've already happened. He's not going anywhere, because He wants to stay right beside me, escort me through this messy life, and one day, take me into a really happy place. In that place, everything does sparkle, my loved ones won't ever get sick or die, and I get to see Him face-to-face and let Him show me a re-cap video of just how present He was in this life of mine.

Sometimes, your baby steps will look much like my temper tantrums. They'll look wrong, messed up, and immature. But when you find yourself all alone and in such a comfortable place with God that you can tell Him exactly where your angry, hurt heart is, you've reached a new level of relationship. There are no more first impressions, no more trying to convince God why He should swipe right on your profile. You just do all the ugly crying and hairbrush throwing you want, because you've learned that rather than testing God's love, you just fall into it and let it ride you through the fire.

That might not feel like progress, but it is. When you figure out the heart of God, that His love is something crazy and beautiful that doesn't bail, you're leaps and bounds closer to seeing that God constantly patches every crack and cranny your lonely heart might feel. He becomes a safe space, Someone you can always count on, even when it's lonely and dark.

# Weird Spaces

I told myself, *I think I'm in hell. Or maybe this is just what hell looks like? If this isn't where I'm at, I guess that's where I'll end up after I leave this place. IF I escape...*

Trapped inside four walls painted blood red and black, swastikas plastered on tapestries and posters with drained liquor bottles falling off every counter, all I could think was *How did I get here?* This definitely wasn't a Peyton kind of place; heck, I still had stuffed bears and toy giraffes in my lavender room.

The first big girl job I landed after earning my BA was as a reporter and writer for *Troup County News*. I got to talk and write, two things a sorority girl with a degree in English dreams of. Not only was this a job I enjoyed, but I couldn't get over how much fun networking and news writing were. A local motorcycle gang was hosting a toy drive during Christmas 2016, and *Troup County News* was invited to take a few pictures and feature their donations. Since this was a weekend gig, the other news reporter and I fought over who had to go. I was the rookie who drew the short stick, so the story became mine.

Preparing for this scary adventure into the unknown, I expected the biker stereotypes: Of course, there would be the black leather, the creepy skulls, and the spiky, dog collar jewelry. I was in for a much longer, scarier, eye-opening ride than that, though. As soon as I pulled up to their clubhouse, all assumptions already confirmed, a man sporting an eyepatch motioned me to park in their grass. When I stepped outside of my car, he introduced himself as "One-eye" and directed me to their hangout. Immediately, I was engulfed by a fog of cigarette smoke, loud, grunting conversations, and a sudden need to find the closest escape route.

I was hoping to be there no longer than 30 minutes, but no, this wasn't where the toy drive was. Lucky me had to ride with one of them, yes, ride on the back of a motorcycle with a complete stranger, to another chapter's clubhouse to take my pictures.

*Great, this won't be a few snaps here, a few quotes there, and I'm home,* I shrugged.

But before I hopped on a motorcycle and held on to one of these gruff transients, I had to pee. Bad.

They invited me inside their clubhouse and motioned toward a room in the back. Tiptoeing into the unknown and waiting my turn for the ladies' room, I slowly looked up and peered at their décor. Skulls, swastikas, more skulls, and even more liquor bottles draped every inch of the place. Assumptions were continuously right.

*Maybe this is a hoax. Maybe there aren't any toys. They're probably waiting until I hole up in the bathroom so they can surround me and sacrifice me upon the backyard woodpile.*

I anticipated my death all day, but no threats were made. No acts of physical violence took place. I didn't even die. And that bathroom was the cleanest bathroom I've ever been in!

My day was safe. I just rode on the back of a motorcycle to another biker clubhouse where I took some pictures and made a few friends. After I realized this would be an all-day affair, I woman-ed up and forced myself to make conversation with these people. Other than a few marijuana offers and a few jail stories, most of the conversation was normal. Once I rode back to the original clubhouse, small-talked my way into my car, and shut the door, I realized how much my life had just changed. Sure, I was impressed with the number of toys they collected; obviously, I was thankful to be alive, but I took home a bigger concept than that. I'm not sure how they tattoo skulls, swastikas, and naked people on their bodies while they also pray to Jesus before their gatherings, but I learned not to judge. I heard their stories, gained a few Facebook friends, and figured out that God puts you in some scary, awkward situations to grow your understanding of Him.

When I went to get in my car and finally head off to normality, One-eye looked at me and said, "If you ever need anything, we've got your back!" Maybe they watched my quick transformation, the way my comfort level shifted throughout the day. Maybe they felt it down in their skull-y bones that I saw them as people. But my heart softened when he spoke. I believed him. I still do.

In Romans 2, Paul is hammering readers with the truth about judging others. In essence, he says, "I don't care if you're outwardly circumcised. I don't care if you are of Jewish descent. If you aren't leading with love, if your heart isn't set on Jesus, the rest is for naught." Sure, skulls, swastikas, and naked people tatoos are not the picture of holiness, but Paul makes it clear that God's central focus is the soul, something no man can see.

When all was said and done, when the paper needed an article and everyone else wanted to know the gossip of a motorcycle gang, I had two options: I could spout off about their heretical interior design skills, or brag on their humble prayer and desire to help children in need. I chose the latter. I did that because I felt who they were as people. Once I erased my fear and had the courage to sit down beside one of these people and talk about life, it became clear that they were just a more inked version of any other human. As humans, in a motorcycle gang or not, we each have a rap sheet that's miles and miles long, but God chooses to see His Son when He looks at us. He takes the best possible version of us and forgets the rest. That's more than we could ever ask for, and even more than we deserve.

God gave us the gift of discovering, creating, and asking questions, but with that curiosity comes a need to know why even the bad things happen, why the awkward things happen, why the things we never saw coming happen. I think that's why we're so apt to ask, "How on earth did I end up here?" We find ourselves in situations that are out of our control, situations we didn't ask for, when all we want is out. But if we take just five minutes to swallow pride, self-righteousness, anger, frustration, and even the need for an upfront explanation, we can find God's peace that navigates us through the impossible places. It usually involves a change of our hearts, a change of our perspective, a shift in our reality. And I promise, it's always for the better.

When I think about people who held tight to this truth, despite the hard stuff, I always think of my man Tim Tebow. He won the Heisman, the pinnacle of success in the South Eastern Conference football world, but his dream to go pro was short-lived. Tossed around from team to team, second-string here, third-string there, he was eventually shoved out of the NFL and never invited back. Announcers made a joke of him, coaches labeled him inept, and he was never enough for the crowds. His good boy name was like a target on his back; the more he returned negative criticism with positive feedback, the more he was lambasted. He was doing everything right, saying everything right, and always making his moves for the right reasons. It was as if he was too genuine for television. The more he boasted in Jesus, the more he paid respect to his naysayers, the more they despised him. It was a sad drama to see unfold as he was displaced from his big dream.

But do you follow this guy on Instagram? On Facebook, Twitter, on any other social media platform? He's not tossing around the good ol' pigskin, but he's still making bold moves for the Gospel. He's making the best of a crushed dream, all because he hung on through the bad times. No doubt, he had the "How did I get here?" moments. I'm sure he felt like a second-rate loser when he saw tabloids, heard commentators, and showed up to games, just to warm a bench. But instead of looking at the problem, listening to the harsh words, he focused on the other opportunities around him, and that's where his eternal contentment stems from. The dude is happy, no doubt. I'm willing to bet he wouldn't trade his ministries and new opportunities for a Super Bowl Championship any day, all because this new fulfillment is worth a huge, intervening change of plans.

\*\*\*

At 26, Peyton was supposed to have her life together. After all, Peyton was the valedictorian, the college virgin, and the very put-together wife. She wasn't supposed to have a mental disorder, a marriage crisis, and a murky, unclear future, especially not all at once. But there I was, in a weird, sad, unexpected, lonely place, a place that included, and still includes, lots of financial debt, and lots of missed opportunities. This place includes lots of reverse roles, lots of not buying the house and not having the baby right after marriage, because we're still in the waiting phase, in the let's-get-to-the-career-goal phase. That doesn't leave room for much conversation regarding purchasing a nice house and affording an endless supply of diapers. This phase includes lots of mess-ups that can't be hidden behind a tidied report card or the singular shining star of sexual purity. Life is much stickier than that now, and I'm slowly realizing it's impossible to totally have life together. We can make things easier by walking with Jesus and letting Him work on us, but in these finite, selfish bodies, we will inevitably stumble and constantly drop the ball.

Easier said than done to walk with Jesus every day, I know. And yeah, there are still hard days, days when living in a one-bedroom apartment and admitting I've been a bratty wife don't feel good. There are days when I feel like God skipped over me in the big, spiritual gifts department, days when I think that this is all just a test of patience, days when I feel like this is all a joke. What I'm learning on these days, though, is that while our feelings can be a beautiful, compelling thing, sometimes they can scatter the truth in one-million different directions.

I believe humans can be super driven by emotions. We don't always trust our sense of logic, our parents, our past experiences, our God, but we're usually gung-ho for trusting our emotions. Honestly, while I think God gave us the gift of feeling moments, feeling people, and feeling feelings, I don't think it's always the smartest decision to base truth on immediate emotional reactions. If you're asking for my advice, I generally avoid my emotions during my decision-making process. I'm trying this new art of trusting my God heart, a heart led by God and not self, and not my emotions. Those two can be hard to separate, but my heart is where Scripture and God speak to me; my emotions are where anger, hurt, and too much excitement compel me to make quick decisions.

On the flip side, emotions compel us to kiss our husbands, cuddle our babies, hug our sad friends. Emotions tend to start revolutions, earth-shaking movements, the big stuff that history can't hide. And with such a delicate, but driving force, we should be careful. We can put out another person's fire with our careless actions, or with our too-careful, cutting words. We can also spark the wrong fire and burn out something good. When we don't treat others' emotions with the same heavy responsibility that we give to our student loans, we've missed out on our purpose. This all goes back to making decisions with your God heart. Let the truth of God guide your feelings, map out what compels you to make decisions, and lead how quickly or slowly you make a choice.

When your heart and emotions are anchored in truth, you have a dynamic duo in the making. Sudden, weird, hard times, like being all by yourself for months, are not the cruel chance for loneliness to showcase the worst parts of you. Isolation can no longer serve as the breeding ground for bitterness. The fear of being alone holds no weight. You're able to serve others, because you can now relate with them. Empathy now has space, because you have the emotions. And you also have the truth of your situation, and God's truth is always the victory, the happy ending, the forever safe space when things don't always feel happy. That's when unbelievers can say, "I'm not sure what she's got, but whatever it is, I want it for myself."

We learn to make peace with the "How did I get here?" questions. True, those identical words will float in and out of our lives with each new stage, each new challenge, each new defeat that comes our way, but this is when we grow. This is when we see a little less problem and a little more people, because maybe we're made to realize that isolation is a choice sometimes, whether we admit it or not. Fear, not God, keeps us bottled up in ourselves. We are to blame for shoving ourselves in the corner, for forgetting what it's like to put ourselves out there and connect with people. Maybe God uses our loneliness as the necessary tool to make us feel the right weight of sadness or stress. And that will push us to do anything to get us out of the house and around others.

Honestly, since when has growing with others been such a terrible thing anyway?

# Tombstone Talks

I roll my eyes at pastors a lot, not that I'm a pastor hater. There are so many men, women, and even children of God who know Him so well that it ministers to me just to be near them. But lots of pastors and church leaders, in general, sling around churchy sayings for the sake of saying the churchy thing, not the Jesus thing, and that is not always right. They powder the truth to look so pretty, with acronyms, rhyme schemes, and cultural trends, that we think there must be something wrong with us when the truth gets ugly and we don't know what to do with it.

My eyes roll and my stomach twists when a pastor stands behind the pulpit to perform a funeral and starts his speech with, "Today is not a day of sadness, but of celebration..."

> *No, today is a day of sadness,* I think. *Can you not see? Can you not feel the weight of pure emptiness and sadness the family on the front row is feeling? Do you not see their tears? Their slouched, shaking shoulders? The angry husband? The downtrodden wife? The numb brothers and sisters? The confused children?*

Yes, we are beyond grateful when we have that deep, deep peace that our loved one is in the most beautiful place with our beautiful Savior. But down here, there's hurt, and it's never been our place to put empathy aside for the sake of hiding behind, "God doesn't give us more than we can handle." Because He will forever give us more than we can handle, if only to prove the beautiful collision of His power, love, and promise that He will forever bring us through things meant to consume us.

For now, on earth, there's grief. And as believers, we have every right to be sad, to hurt, to ache, to throw hairbrushes in anger, to ask questions saturated in pain, to weep so hard, so loud that we can barely breathe, let alone feel anything. After all, Jesus has never been afraid of our humanity. In fact, it's something He was so in love with, and still is, that His whole Godhood is wrapped up in that one time He came down here to get on our level, to walk in our shoes, to connect with us, and save us.

That's why Jesus showed up after Lazarus died. I mean, He's God. It's not like He didn't know when the man was going to die. As the God of every-thing, He had all authority to show up and keep Lazarus alive if He had wanted to, but Jesus chose to let him face death and to let Lazarus' loved ones grieve first. Not only that, but Jesus chose to sit with Lazarus' loved ones and weep. If I had to bet, I'd guarantee you our Savior's grief was the rawest kind, our kind, with the snotty nose, puffy eyes, quivering lip, and the tears that few men dare to humbly shed.

Not that Jesus enjoys the reality centered on pain, but He sees a beauty in our suffering, the kind of beauty He willingly experienced. Jesus sees the sort of aftermath that means something; He sees the ashes that He will make beautiful. He sees an avenue for bigger, better things, once we face something like death. In Lazarus' case, Jesus wanted to grieve with His people. He wanted us to know He's the kind of God Who isn't afraid to walk through the dark. He isn't the kind of God Who runs when things look black and hopeless.

He has given us the freedom to mourn our loss because that's when He has the space to resurrect us.

Pepa, Curtis Harlon, my grandfather, the love of my life, the John Deere® of John Deeres, the best Elvis Presley impersonator, the only true "Teach Me How To Dougie," master, left this earth unexpectedly. Sure, he was 75, but he was in near-perfect health. There was no cancer, no hardcore diabetes, no weird blood test results. He was fine, always had been. But when a stroke creeps up and throws you into a coma, fate is only God's to decide.

He was in the hospital a few days and was sent to hospice when he remained unresponsive. Hospice is a weird place. It's where the world's best nurses work, a place that restores your opinion of humanity when you watch volun-teers knit quilts to keep patients warm, when you watch military veterans salute your unconscious grandfather and place an honorary certificate at his feet. But meanwhile, it's where I've stood as I've watched some of my favorite people leave this earth. It's where I've seen a 30-year-old man lose his battle with cancer, and a 12-year-old lose it when his young mother was consumed by cancer. It's a place with sights and sounds you want to block out, but never can. It's a place you don't want to be, but when the love of your life is there, you're drawn to this weird environment that operates within the unsteady middle ground between life and death.

The nurses told us they believed Pepa could hear us, understand what we were saying, even in a coma. I wasn't sure if I believed this, but I forced negativity aside long enough to accept the idea. One night, when everyone else had stepped out of the room to get food, take a break, grieve alone, I stayed with him. I pulled my laptop out and pulled Elvis Presley up on Spotify. I blared that music. Lord knows I blared that music.

The nurses also said some coma patients have recovered when certain sounds or memories triggered their brains, so I thought some of his favorite memories of us might wake him up. "Hound Dog" bounced off the whitewashed walls in his hospice room as I grabbed his hands and rocked them back and forth, dancing with him, begging him to open his eyes, begging him not to leave us down here, but it didn't work. His arms fell limp the moment I let go of his aged, calloused hands. Not a twitch, not a flinch anywhere. A deeper part of me thinks he was hearing music, but it was the perfect kind of music played in a realm far, far away, the kind of music created and choreographed by an even better King.

A few days later, Pepa left us for a much prettier place, a place where He could shout God's praises louder than he ever had on this earth. I think Pepa was one of those Christians who was so pure that Peter didn't have to check his name at the gate. I firmly believe, with all the muster and power in me, that Jesus didn't wait for the golden gates to slowly open so He could embrace my Pepa. No, my Jesus used every bit of His perfect power to bend the bars, popping pearls off the gate, to bust through the entrance and tackle Pepa. They were best friends, no doubt. And that will forever be a beautiful legacy, a spiritual brand that my heart will always proudly wear.

I can still feel the sound of the military salvos from those rifles fired at his graveside. The ringing echoed in my heart, bouncing like a destructive pinball, blowing the deepest holes in every piece of me. I cried, I wept, I broke into one-million pieces, wearing my thick, itchy, black dress as a symbol of the utter discomfort of death. And then, after his funeral, in leggings and a sweatshirt big enough to hide me, I felt nothing. For days, I didn't cry, not at night, not in the shower, not when I visited my grandmother. I started feeling guilty, wondering where my grief was, where my humanity had gone. I didn't want to admit the guilt at first, but it was there, replaying shoulda, woulda, coulda's.

I've always been a self-shamer. I've trained myself to see shame as a sign of conviction, a full-blown reminder that the Holy Spirit is with me, even if He's making me feel really bad. But I've mistaken His character; the Holy Spirit's conviction is never meant to shame. It's meant to heal, to make us whole. I hadn't been displaced from my religious hurt long enough to see this, though. Even at 21, I was still terrified of God, justifying His thunderbolts with my failures, assuming His righteousness was attainable, but something He didn't want to share. Scary, right? It's exhausting and downright depressing when I replay this narrative that I trudged through for 13 years.

But now, I know God as the Savior Who has a way of meeting us at the mouth of our biggest fears, in the middle of the scariest, most shattering places, so He can share in our pain and give us the victory too. He's always been the kind of God Who takes the backseat after He's done all the work to give us the win-win scenarios.

The first win is that my Pepa is forever in heaven, a place where I get to see him again. The other win is that I've learned God isn't scared of my humanity. My Pepa's death didn't feel like a victory, but his passing produced this gold-lining in my life; it created this safe space for me to feel human without the threat of God bailing on me. Numbness began to melt when I started visiting Pepa's grave. Tears found their way down my face, and feeling something, even if it was sadness, was a relief.

I found God at the tombstone of the only earthly man who never hurt my heart. God found me six feet under, suffocating in my own hurt. And while I sat and wept, His hands busted with blisters as He stood out in the rain, the cold, the sun, the heat and kept digging to find me, to pull me out of the muck, to let me feel His grace. I felt every bit of Him. I felt Him chunk rocks and trash dead flowers that had clogged my heart from remembering the One Who sees me, the One Who sustains me through my pain.

121

Best part? God wasn't trying to fix my sadness. Instead, He was just sitting with me. He was crying with me. He was on His hands and knees, pulling weeds off the edges of Pepa's tombstone with me. He was hunched over me, above me, His scarred back blocking the Georgia heat so I could straighten up the American flag at Pepa's military marker. He was lying in the grass beside me as I looked up at the sky, wondering if Pepa was looking down at me, seeing me sit right beside his earthly resting place.

Most people visit a grave to mourn the loss of a loved one. In fact, most people avoid graveyards altogether. They have a harsh, somewhat eerie stigma. But me? Now? I'll drive through hell itself to get to that tombstone to talk to my Pepa and feel my God.

There's life at the graveside for me. There's life in loneliness. I would say I don't know how or why but the how is God. The why, is God. The beginning, middle, and end are Him too. And I think it's all because God isn't scared for death and life to meet head-on. After all, our faith hinges on a God Who sent His Son in the flesh, so Life could face death, face its sadness and presumed victory, only to defeat it in the end, for all of us.

But we don't have to wait for a loved one to die, or for the death of anything, to tap into God's life. There are loads of freedom to accept before Jesus comes back. You see, He has every bit of the goodness of life in the palm of His hand, and it's as easy as telling Him you're drowning, your heart and mind are dying, and you need Him and the life He gives.

True, it's a freedom and a contentment that won't always be easy. You'll still walk through some darkness and lots of gray spaces, but you won't be shackled. You won't be chained to the things that seek to choke you and suffocate your identity in Who Jesus is and what He did for you. The bad things might seem like they're winning sometimes, death might be more real than you want to face, but Jesus has given us an out. We won't be the ones slaying the enemy, and most likely, we won't make record time sprinting through the hard stuff. We are free to not be perfect.

Take that in. We are free to *not* be perfect.

Seriously, we are free to stumble and crawl through the hard, scary things, because God has sent His Spirit down here to do the fighting, the protecting, the slaying:

122

*The LORD your God is in your midst, a mighty one who will save; he will rejoice over you with gladness; he will quiet you by his love; he will exult over you with loud singing.*
Zephaniah 3:17

He's the ultimate Lover and Fighter. He has forever mastered the art of facing down darkness with the purest love that drives every demon away, every lonely lie away, every bad doctor's note, every death, every separation, every loss, every question that was never answered. And He does it while singing. He has every confidence in His skills and ability to put us before Himself.

Everything bad, everything ugly, everything hopeless, no longer has a grip on you. In Jesus' name, you are free. You are free to feel, free to be numb, free to lay down when the darkness is too much, free to stand on God's own two feet, knowing that you are forever free because the weight of sin and darkness isn't on your shoulders. Jesus took care of that big burden thousands of years ago. Because of Him, you are free to breathe a sigh of relief, free to rest in the biggest messes.

You're free. It's not a temporary thing. It's not something that will be taken away after so many mess-ups. Your freedom is a freedom that parallels the goodness of Jesus throughout eternity. But I think Jesus says it best:

*Take off the grave clothes...* John 11:44 (NIV)

Take them off because there's life underneath the tatters, shreds, and stains. There's no need to trip over the loose strips. There's no need to wear the thick stench as a form of punishment, a means to justify the wrong you've done, or the pain you've experienced.

You're already resurrected, never to taste death. You can't lose. Not now, not ever.

Take that in again: You are free to not be perfect for all eternity.

# A Good Pandemic

One of the hardest bouts of OCD I've faced, and continue to face, is Contamination OCD. This isn't a tricky one. In short, my brain can trace back everything that has touched everything, recollecting the worst possible contamination zones. As with most forms of OCD, the fixations stem from a childhood trauma or a harsh life experience. When I was in the second grade, a fourth-grade student at my school passed away. He was sick with something like the flu. His poor body couldn't fight it off and process all the medicine he was taking, so he went to be with Jesus. At seven years old, I couldn't process how people got sick, let alone died. All I knew was that germs made you sick. If germs could make someone at my school die, then I could die. I had to keep the germs away.

By the time I was in fourth grade, I had given myself eczema. It's not an uncommon skin condition, and it's nothing fatal. It's just an intense, constant battle of dry skin that can result in cracks and bleeding and sandpaper skin. But rather than my body producing this issue on its own, I gave it to myself from going through globs of sanitizer. I used so much sanitizer that people started giving it to me as a present. I got about 20 bottles of sanitizer for Christmas one year. People had also memorized my favorite brands of sanitizer. I preferred the blue raspberry and purple grape foaming sanitizer from Bath & Body Works®. They don't sell it anymore, so don't feel obligated to send any to me.

If you can picture snaggle-toothed, freckle-faced, tangle-haired Peyton with cracking, bleeding hands at age ten, I dare you to visualize me locked up in my house in a global pandemic. I've never had time for germs, and I really don't have the mental capacity for them amidst Covid-19.

Let's get real, I don't like capitalizing the "c" in "Covid." I'm tired of this virus stomping around and being a bully, tired of it thinking it has power over me, my family, my friends, my coworkers, the world. While this is quite the tough gal mantra, Covid bullies me because I let it. It's the kid who stalks my locker, knowing I'm always the first one to hand over my lunch money.

I'm like most of society amidst this pandemic. I wear my mask. I use hand sanitizer. I use more hand sanitizer. And, oh yeah, I use even more hand sanitizer. I stay away from groups and people in general. But OCD takes these CDC measurements and puts them on steroids:

When the state of Georgia first went on lockdown, when I was able to work from home, I washed my hands about 57 times in a day. I think it was 57. I lost track. And the fact I took the time to count how many times I washed my hands is its own form of obsession.

No shoes were allowed in the house. If Josh had to wear his nice leather shoes to work, too bad! Those jokers were sleeping outside. After all, I couldn't determine if Josh had carried the virus home on his shoes. And if he did come in with his shoes on, I felt the need to mop.

Within a week of lockdown, I gave myself dermatitis, a.k.a., a scratchy, patchy, stinging rash. I would wash my hands a lot, but I was also afraid that my hands might touch the inside of the sink while I was washing them, thus contaminating my hands all over again. So, instead of facing the sink and rinsing the soap off my hands, I'd lather them up and then wipe them off on a towel. All of this antibacterial soap would cling to my skin since I didn't wash it off, and it would soak itself into my wrists. Then *boom*! Big rash breakout.

I wouldn't eat takeout from my favorite restaurants for a month, and that's sad. Even drive-thrus made me nervous. How many people's credit cards had they touched by the time their gloves messed with my stuff?

The kitchen freaked me out. This is where my food was. This is the place that's always supposed to be clean. One night, I was trying to cook beef strog-anoff. I browned the meat, washed my hands a lot, tried to get a pan out of the bottom kitchen cabinet, couldn't tell if the pan touched the floor, where I hadn't recently mopped, and then it was a total anxiety attack. First, I took my wooden spoon and whacked it against the kitchen counter, furious that I would have to wash another pan for what I low-key knew was no decent reason. Next, I sobbed. I sobbed and I sobbed and I sobbed because I was so tired of germs and always trying to keep track of what touched what and I just couldn't take it anymore. Last, Josh was a total champ and finished cooking dinner for me.

Walking the dogs became a big stressor because I didn't want to wear a mask for their one-mile walk in Georgia in July, but I would pass too many people along the way. Already cranky from heat and a muggy mask, tension would rise when I spotted a cigarette butt or a used napkin in the grass. How old was the cigarette butt? It can take up to 72 hours for Covid to die on surfaces. Who used that napkin? Did it just fly out of someone's car before it could be used? Or did somebody blow their frickin' nose in it? And why did Daisy just eat that cigarette butt? She's not licking me for at least three days. So, walks became total chaos.

Three months after lockdown, once restrictions were lifted, I went back to work. I've been back at work for about four weeks now and I'm the only person in my office who has went through their entire bottle of company-given hand sanitizer. I'm almost finished with my second bottle now. But it's okay. I have five more bottles of the stuff stored away in my kitchen.

In case you don't get the picture, I'm a constant wreck. If I'm not dodging cigarette butts, I'm washing my hands with closed eyes and retracted lips so water from the inside of the sink can't pop out and hit my face. When I'm not panicking about cooking, I'm murdering my bladder, refusing to use the public restroom at work when I really have to go.

I'm not sure how many of you are struggling with my same germ-infestation problem, but Covid is kicking butt and taking names in other ways too. People have lost loved ones over this. People have medical bills stacked sky-high, paying for fighting this. People haven't seen their loved ones in months. Fear and loneliness are unavoidable. You've faced and still battle at least one of them, whether you admit it or not. Honestly, I think we don't like to admit when we're scared or lonely, because the instant we say it, it's real. And then we have to do something with it.

When Covid first hit, I hadn't been to therapy for a while. Josh had been home for a few months and my brain had slowed down, but even when the virus broke out and I could feel my Contamination OCD rising, I pushed off therapy. I didn't want to spend the money and I didn't want to start this process all over. But about a month into lockdown, I couldn't take it. I had to talk to a professional.

What my therapist has taught me is that I put lots of pressure on myself. When I dump my latest issue on her, she always wants me to see it "with love and compassion." Therapy is usually an hour of me forcing myself to give myself grace. Giving yourself grace sounds like a sweet release, but since I walk such a tightrope and expect others to do the same, grace almost turns into a guilt trip. While I might be justified in giving myself grace amidst a pandemic, that's no excuse for me to be mad at Josh when he's tired of my mandates that he wash his hands 57 times in a day too. While it might not always seem like I care when I put people under my OCD pressures, I do. And it breaks my heart.

I'm not sure if you've watched *The Chosen*, but it's the biggest fan-funded tv series ever. It's about the life of Jesus, and before you pass it off as some stoic documentary, listen up: This show is good! For the first time in multimedia, Jesus feels relatable. He isn't floating around town and speaking the King James. He's meeting people where they are, dancing at weddings, winking to fill in awkward conversations, and chewing on straw. In short, this show reveals that God's love is radical enough to stoop to earth in the name of human connection and relationships. Want to know something cool? With my job at Giving Company, and as content managers, my coworker and I were able to interview the guy who plays Jesus, Peter's wife, Eden, the director, and associate director, and one of the pharisees, Shmuel. (It's pronounced ShmooEL. Please watch the interview as I, a Georgia girl, and my Alabama coworker try to properly say the Hebrew word for Samuel. It's beyond entertaining.)

The interview with the cast member playing Jesus was off the chart. I'm sure that's not a shock. But the interview that broke me apart in all the good ways was with Shaan Sharma, who plays Shmuel.

Of course, these interviews happened via Zoom, thanks to Covid, but my coworker and I hopped on a call with Shaan to talk about the tension and emotion he had to emulate playing a pharisee. While these are basic character sketch questions, the conversation took a convicting turn. I'm summarizing here, but Shaan turned a question around for me and my coworker: How many of us have been raised to believe a certain way, and we grow up believing we're right, only to find out we're wrong? And how often does the fear of being wrong keep us from the truth?

I didn't want to interview anymore. I wanted to curl up in a ball in an empty cubicle and cry.

Truth is, I've wondered what choice I would've made if I had been on earth when Jesus came. I'm always so set in the comfort zone and instant justification of rules that I would've wrestled to accept why Jesus came to earth so differently than anticipated. We hold the beauty of 2,000 years' worth of hindsight. We know Jesus is the Messiah. He's God's Son. He came down here for 33 years, mopped the tomb's floor clean, and busted out of sin's grave, so for all of eternity, man has hope. I know that. I've accepted Jesus. I'm obsessed with always chasing Him down. But I also know that it might not have been so easy for me, had I been a random civilian in 30 AD.

And I finally admitted that to Shaan in the interview, for thousands of people to watch. I said it. And do you know what he said to me a few minutes later in the interview? He said, "Don't be hard on yourself." He didn't say, "Don't be so hard on yourself." He didn't sneak the "so" in there to make me feel as if I still needed to take boxing gloves to my face. He extended God's grace to me so I didn't have to fight normal human questions. God got to be God. I got to be a human. And for someone with Religious OCD, someone who fights obsessing over rules and safety and spiritual contamination, this is something to hang onto when days get hard.

Let's be honest, days are really hard for most of us right now, especially with Covid looming over our heads, clogging up our newsfeed, and keeping us isolated. We're either struggling mentally, emotionally, financially, physically, or spiritually, and to be honest, I'm struggling in all of those ways.

When life takes a nosedive that I didn't prep for, I'm always afraid it's some sort of punishment. Sure, that stems from growing up in a church that portrayed God as a Zeus-like character who threw thunderbolts for fun, but it's still a real part of my journey with Jesus. It's one of those uphill paths full of loose rock and sneaky holes that I refuse to give up on.

Most of the time, the roadblocks on the path are lies that God doesn't stay. That in the middle of this chaos, in the middle of my mess-ups, He leaves. I mean, can you blame Him? I know I wouldn't blame Him for being fed up with thousands of years of selfishness and ignorance. But my prayer for almost a year, the "God, just stay" prayer, continues to be my mantra. Want to know something even cooler about "God, just stay"? Look it up in Hebrew. But before you look up the Hebrew, you need to know that for years, I've wanted a tattoo. Hang with me:

Maybe it's because my father is covered in them, or maybe it's a Millennial thing; we get blamed for being bad crazies anyway. But deep down, I think I want a Jesus tattoo as a physical reminder that He won't leave. Surely, if I ink His name into my skin, He won't leave me. When I was looking up the translation for "My God stays," I noticed something. There's no direct translation for "My God stays." The real translation in Hebrew? "God remains."

God is so God that He doesn't need my personal possessive pronoun in front of His name to still rule me and all the cosmos. God doesn't need to stay; He wants to remain. And there's a difference. Staying is strained. It's holding on with a worn grip. It's the kind of staying that I did when my ex-boyfriend always had another girl on the side. It's the kind of staying when a former boss overworked and underpaid me, a young kid who couldn't even afford medical insurance.

Let it sink in: God doesn't need to stay; He wants to remain.

If you look up the definition of "remains," it means: the parts left over after other parts have been removed, used, or destroyed. Yes, I know there's a verb/noun difference in definitions here, but here's the thing: God doesn't just stay. He remains when everything around us is snatched up, abused, and left for ruin. Even when we are the ones to blame for the ash pile around us, He stays. Even when we had nothing to do with the chaos of a pandemic, He stays.

I'm not sure I'll ever fully wrap my heart around this truth on this side of heaven, because I know that OCD doesn't plan on packing up and moving out of my brain. But the good thing is that truth doesn't hinge on my weakness. It hinges on His power, His mercy, and His love that never needed my weakness or loneliness but wanted it instead.

I can't be by myself because of Him. And for that, I'll forever chase Him down.

# Back Home

From the get-go, we didn't know how long Josh would have to be away; it was just a waiting game that had me holding my breath, which was agony when I constantly wanted to cry at the same time. Regardless, nearly four months had felt like centuries. I'm positive that this experience put my crow's feet on steroids, so it was a relief when the four months were up and Josh was able to come home for good. Honestly, I don't think "relief" quite covers the feeling.

An airport near our house opened a flight instructing job and he was able to transfer to Georgia. At first, Josh thought he would surprise me with the news, but he's terrible with surprises. Bless Josh's soul, he was no good at keeping our engagement a secret, either. For starters, he's never been one to make me feel obligated to hang out with him, in dating and in marriage. If I want to go rogue without sharing much detail, he's always cool with giving me my space, free of texts, phone calls, and the like. But one day, he was hell-bent on me blocking out an entire Saturday to go hiking with him. He made me cancel a shopping trip with a friend, which had never happened, so already, I knew something was up. Then, magically, a few days before the hike, he wanted to go on a day-trip with my father so they could "hang out." A few days later, my sister forced me to get a manicure with her. I don't do manicures. I have Contamination OCD and manicures usually gross me out.

In summary: I have to hang out with him all day Saturday. He's just spent eight hours of "bro time" with my father. And I've been forced to get a manicure. Then the poor guy picks me up to go hiking and forgets that the ring

131

box is bulging out of his right khaki shorts pocket. Needless to say, I had to act surprised when he got down on one knee and popped out my grandmother's beautiful ring.

Switching back to his next biggest failed surprise, Josh said he was only coming home for the weekend, just to visit for a few days, but I found his twin-sized bedspread hidden under the staircase in the basement, and it didn't take five seconds for me to put two and two together. Mom also ratted him out. So, I kept waiting for him to spill the news, and he was taking his precious, sweet time. Josh came home on a Thursday night and didn't say a word then, not Friday, not Saturday, not Sunday, not Monday morning when he was supposed to leave. Finally, before I left for work Monday morning, I marched into our bedroom and demanded that he tell me what was going on. He wanted to play dumb, be goofy at first, which is what he does best, but I didn't have the emotional capacity to joke at this point. I told him the clues I'd found and the secrets I knew, and then he had no other option but to tell me what was going on.

I'm pretty sure I cried when he confirmed my happy suspicions that he was home to stay, but I'm positive that I nearly collapsed. Exhaustion and stress alleviated and my body felt light and free. It. Was. Over.

The sleeping by myself was over. Checking the basement at two in the morning was over. The cooking dinner on Monday and eating the leftovers for days was over. Paying bills, visiting the dog park, watching tv by myself, all were over. I was on Cloud 9, and my feet were floating. My life was no longer "fine," "okay," and "just hanging in there." My life was good.

Much to my surprise, that high didn't last long. The internal hell wasn't over. But truth be told, I shouldn't have been surprised.

I remember one of those really intense mirror talks with God that I had only a few weeks before Josh came home for good. I was doing the kind of praying that happens in your head, the kind with so many emotions and words swirling around at once that you ask God to make sense of them. I was mad, sad, confused, and scared. I didn't want to have a positive outlook. I wanted Josh home. I knew I shouldn't have been acting this way, but it felt good to be acting this way. But I really, really knew I shouldn't have been acting this way. I kind of took all these things, piled them up, and gently shoved them in front of God, hoping and praying He would just take it all and make me better.

I was crying, the angry crying. It was the chest aching, shoulders tensing, nose flaring crying. The kind of crying that only comes from a place of raw, real hurt. My hands gripped the sides of the bathroom sink while my face tilted up to the mirror, staring at the mascara smudges smearing underneath my eyes and the nasty snot clogging my nose. When I had enough of my haggard reflection, I tilted my head back down, staring at the bottom of the sink, distracting myself with how clean I kept the four little porcelain walls.

Deep down, I knew God wanted to use this time to change me, or at least that's how He wanted me to use this time. I, on the other hand, preferred to kill this time with reminding Josh of how much he'd put me through. I just hoped God was okay with letting me pitch habitual fits.

But that was wrong, and very, very selfish.

I'm 100 percent convinced that when I was having that mirror meltdown, God confirmed that I hadn't learned anything the whole time. Actually, I had learned things, but I was in no mood to apply them to my life. At this point in the game, I'd have to go back and tell my mom, dad, sister, grandmother, and even worse, Josh, that I had been wrong, that I had handled this season like a brat.

So why did He let Josh come home while I was too stubborn to grow? I think it was because Jesus wanted me to realize that Josh was never the one who could/would fix my lonely little mess. I had to realize that sometimes, the only way I grow is when I grow disgusted with my spiritual stagnation.

I think Jesus enjoys using the obnoxious parts of our personalities for our good, even when we don't know it. Jesus knows I'm competitive, that I can't take a simple church softball game lightly, that I can't lose at Spades if I'm playing against Josh. I don't even spend my Starbucks stars when I have enough points to get a free drink or free coffee mug; I just have an obsession with beating each challenge on the app. When I forget to scan my app on the deadline, I get upset. It seriously bothers me. When another church beats our church at softball, I get mad, especially if the other Jesus softball team doesn't act like Him. I feel the boiling bubbles spill up and down my hands, arms, and shoulders. My toes curl, my fingers clench, and I grit my teeth. I'm not sure if it's God wanting to use this for justice, or if it's sin that wants to fuel my false righteousness, but I feel bred to compete, to win, to prove what's right, and trump everything else.

It's easy to justify my temper by thinking that my personality parallels Peter's, one of Jesus' biggest, baddest disciples, but Peter's temper was exactly why Peter cut people's ears off and bucked Paul's willingness to free Jews and Gentiles from the rigid rituals of the law. Peter's temper was exactly what Jesus challenged and changed.

But let's assume my hopes and dreams of being a female Peter are valid and that I'm bred solely to compete, then you best bet that I take losses personally. They don't settle with me. They stop me at the bleachers, in the middle of kitchen chores, or even writing this book. I just don't like taking the "L." I pair losses with failures and, as an accurately-assumed perfectionist, losses cause an identity crisis.

Cool enough, even if I just like the tough idea of being called to be a competitor and it's not even a Jesus thing, He uses my preferred alter ego to His advantage, which in return is always to my advantage too. Because God's just that kind. If I fail big, especially in the spiritual realm, Jesus knows I'll be ripping and roaring the next morning, jumping out of bed determined to help God slay my own sin. Granted, His resurrection is what has already annihilated my sin, but I think Jesus appreciates my efforts too. So, when I handled the first go-round of Josh being gone like a total punk, using God's kindness to my advantage when I wanted the world, especially Josh, to feel bad for me, He thought round two might be a little more spiritually advantageous for me.

Funny thing is, when I started writing this book, Josh had been home a few months. I first typed out a few of these inspirational ideas one day at work. I had a different title, different approach, but the subtle calling was the same. I came home from work one day and told Josh that I needed to write this book about loneliness and where God was in the middle of it all, and Josh was my biggest cheerleader to bring it to life. Covid gave me the time to bring a story to each chapter, and only one week after I received the contract to have this baby published, Josh moved to Auburn, Alabama to be a flight instructor there.

In April, when Covid was hitting airlines hard, Josh was let go from his former flight instructor's job, so like the maddest madwoman ever, I was applying him for more flight jobs. I mean, he needed the hours and we needed the money, so did location even matter? There was Montana, the Dakotas, and Illinois. Then there was Florida, Alabama, and Kansas, even Alaska. You name a state, and you best bet I sent in a cover letter, resume, and piloting documentation.

Auburn University? I applied him there, so this round two thing would leave no one to blame but me. I was that desperate to get him back on his feet, to make sure we had running water and dog food for the pups. It was a while before anyone called him for an interview. After all, no one was too excited to fly at this time, so when Auburn offered him the job, I did what any good wife does a second time. I said, "Okay, let's do this."

But the "let's" looked a little different. It wasn't just me and Josh facing this bout again. It was me, Josh, and Jesus. The first time Josh was gone, I just thought it was Jesus letting Josh get his hours. Now, I know it's about more than flight hours. It's about Him saying, "Okay, Peyton, ready to let me start breaking you? Ready to watch me shift and change the shards and pieces? Ready to come out of your rueful, rule-full shell? Ready to just let go, love, and be loved?"

I know that's what He said. Or something very similar. I chuckled and said what every "good" Christian says, "Okay, God. Let's do this! But do we actually have to do this again? Is this just a post-test? I know I mentioned a round two boxing ring in the beginning of my book and all, but I'm good with one and done."

Forever a good girl, I'd never really had to practice what I preached, but now, now that I've been through the hard stuff and am no longer "perfect," now that I've written a book about seeing God's goodness when you're alone, I get to live that.

Can I be honest and tell you I don't want to have to live out this part?

Can I be even more honest and tell you I just got off the phone with my mom and said I didn't want to do this again?

Can I be the honest of honest and tell you I have tears caking themselves on my face right now as I'm writing this?

135

Can I tell you I'm exhausted?

Can I tell you I'm lonely?

Can I tell you my heart feels like it's breaking again?

I'm sitting in a lonely apartment, living out this story. I'm back to watching tv by myself, making a big pizza casserole on Monday and surviving on it for the rest of the week. I'm back to randomly walking from the tiny living room to the even tinier bedroom, then walking back again. I'm back to turning on my Jesus nightlight that's shaped like a cross and taking forever to get comfortable in our bed by myself. I flip and flop on pillows, forget I'm supposed to eat, and count down the days until the weekend so I can at least see my family.

Is it just as hard as the first time? Yes, in so many ways, especially when battling my OCD. I'm probably wrong, but I've decided that OCD is the thorn in my side. It's the one thing I will forever drag through this life, the one thing that will always make me care more for Jesus and heaven than for this earthly place. And perhaps that's why He lets us struggle with some wars that we will forever wage as we balance the good and bad of life.

But even with this tornado of pain, can I tell you that God is good?

Can I tell you He sits with me in the dark, when hurt and fear stifle my mind?

Can I tell you that I can feel His presence bottling up my tears, both the happy and sad ones?

Can I tell you I hear Him louder when I'm alone?

Can I tell you I feel Him making me a better human, even when He's cramming shards and pieces of my heart in their rightful place, bruising and cutting me where I need to be open and exposed?

Can I tell you, deep down, I feel safe?

Can I tell you I've never felt Him louder than when I've felt free to cuss at Him and throw hair brushes when I don't hear Him as loudly as I want?

Can I tell you He's my Daddy?

Can I tell you He's my Best Friend?

Can I tell you He is head over heels for you, even the parts of you that make you hate yourself?

Can I tell you, because He's that good, you're not so by yourself?

Don't believe me? I totally get it. Thanks to a mental disorder, I can't believe 75 percent of my own thoughts, but I dare you to believe Him. Ask Him the hard questions; listen to the hard, sometimes vague answers. And believe. Please believe, even when the answer isn't clear. Believe He's so good that you will never be left.

It's forever worth it-- on earth and in heaven.

# ABOUT
# KHARIS PUBLISHING

**KHARIS PUBLISHING** is an independent, traditional publishing house with a core mission to publish impactful books, and channel proceeds into establishing mini-libraries or resource centers for orphanages in developing countries, so these kids will learn to read, dream, and grow. Every time you purchase a book from Kharis Publishing or partner as an author, you are helping give these kids an amazing opportunity to read, dream, and grow. Kharis Publishing is an imprint of Kharis Media LLC. Learn more at https://www.kharispublishing.com.

Made in the USA
Monee, IL
01 September 2021